EXECUTIVE DECISION MAKING

McKINSEY FOUNDATION LECTURE SERIES

Sponsored by the
Graduate School of Business, Columbia University

EXECUTIVE DECISION MAKING

Observations and Experience in Business and Government

MARION B. FOLSOM
Director and Management Adviser, Eastman Kodak Company
Former Secretary of the Department of Health,
Education, and Welfare

McGraw-Hill Book Company, Inc.
NEW YORK   TORONTO   LONDON   1962

PREFACE

The management of large organizations is the continuing subject of the lecture series sponsored jointly by the Columbia Graduate School of Business and the McKinsey Foundation for Management Research, Inc. The accumulating volumes resulting from this series have added significantly to our knowledge of the thinking and policies of those charged with chief executive responsibility for managing large organizations.

Two major aspects of the subject have captured the interest of Mr. Marion B. Folsom in this publication. First, he examines some of the assignments that staff organizations can perform most effectively in management's primary task of making decisions and establishing policies. Second, he discusses the nature of policy determination in large business firms and in the executive branch of the federal government. As he does this, he suggests areas where one group might learn from the other.

In an economy in which the institutions are mixed among private and public, we need to supplement what is known about policy formation in one area with that which has been found out so painstakingly in another. From his long experience in highly responsible positions in both business and the federal government, Mr. Folsom is uniquely capable to provide for us an explanation and analysis of the similarities and differences of executive action in the two areas.

He joined the Eastman Kodak Company in 1914, served as assistant to founder George Eastman during the 1920's, and was company treasurer from 1935 to 1953, when he resigned to become Under Secretary of the U. S. Treasury. At the same time, he has served on numerous local, state, and federal advisory committees, including executive or advisory capacities under all four federal Administrations since 1934. He was, for example, a member of the council that helped to draw up the Social Security Act of 1935. In addition, Mr. Folsom has served as chairman of the Committee for Economic Development and a director of the Federal Reserve Bank of New York.

In the long history of the development of American corporations, and especially in recent years, the decision-making function has deservedly received considerable attention. Policy determination and decision making is by no means all that concerns the men responsible for the welfare of large organizations. However, in a world marked by rapid growth and change, planning and decision making are at the center of their attention.

Mr. Folsom analyzes the decision process as it is now commonly practiced in large organizations. In his view, a major reason for the increased productivity of the American economy has been the development and proper use of qualified staffs to aid the planning and decision work of both business firms and government. Among the areas of staff work described by Mr. Folsom are sales forecasting, budgeting, industrial relations, recruitment and training of executives, market research, and industrial research. These are examples of areas in which chief executives and their closely associated officers need the assistance provided by competent staff. They cannot safely be left to the occasional attention of operating executives or to the intuitive judgment of the leaders of the organization.

Governments—particularly on the state and local levels—might learn much from business firms about the effective use of staff and about its ability to aid wise and informed decisions. One way in which businessmen can assist the governmental decision process is to help to make further staff work available—by serving on advisory councils, by helping to finance municipal research bureaus, by testifying at legislative hearings, and by encouraging legislators to provide permanent staffs for their major committees.

Improved staff work in local governments is one of a variety of possible benefits cited by Mr. Folsom that could result from a more thorough understanding by both business and government executives of each other's decision processes. The street is two-way. Business firms might well benefit, for example, from a study of the federal Executive Department's budgeting procedures, and of the processes of persuasion in government as they contribute to effective implementation of decisions.

Corporations, moreover, could benefit from greater use of so-called task forces to study important problems. Men from outside the departments immediately involved—with their more objective viewpoints—are often in a position to make valuable suggestions. The federal government has greatly benefited from commissions made up of men of various backgrounds who bring in fresh viewpoints.

We are fortunate to have Mr. Folsom's explanation of the work of a Cabinet Secretary and of the use by various Presidents of their Cabinets and their White House staffs. The contrasts in executive "styles" from President Theodore Roosevelt to President Kennedy are interesting examples of the adaptation of decision processes and decision-making organizations to each of the Presidents' individual personalities, and to the different situations which each faced. We also are provided with an insight of different ways in which Secretaries have approached the organization and direction of their Departments. Thus Mr. Folsom has provided for us not only some general ideas about decision making in government but also an explanation of the necessity and means for varying the decision process according to the changing requirements. The same necessity is presumably applicable to business.

This book is based on three lectures which Mr. Folsom first presented as the sixth McKinsey lecturer to a group of prominent businessmen and scholars on the Columbia campus. The original lectures have been considerably expanded and modified. Some of the additional thoughts were taken from the informal dinner discussions which followed each lecture, but most of the added material has been newly developed by Mr. Folsom for this book. Editorial collaboration was provided by Professor James P. Logan of the Columbia Business School and by Mr. J. Franklin Teegardin and Mr. Russell L. Olson of the Eastman Kodak Company.

COURTNEY C. BROWN
Dean, Graduate School of Business
Columbia University

CONTENTS

EXECUTIVE DECISION MAKING

I

DECISION MAKING IN A BUSINESS ORGANIZATION

At the end of the first decade of this century Harvard President Charles W. Eliot, in composing the citation for the degree given by the university's newly established Graduate School of Business Administration, referred to business as "the oldest of the arts and the youngest of the professions."

His remarks characterized management generally—not only management in business, but in government Departments and agencies, and the White House. In those days the success of executives depended to a large extent upon their arriving at sound decisions by intuition. To the extent that intuition continues as a major factor in decision making, management will remain an art.

But surely the technique of management has come a long way since then, and this is particularly true of management's number-one function—that of making decisions and establishing policies.

We often think of decision making as something done by a single person acting alone—the president of a company or someone else in the line organization. And it is true that the executive responsible for a given matter must decide among various proposed courses of action and must then stand behind his decision. There is, however, a great deal more to the decision-making process.

Decisions generally are the result of a long series of discussions by both line and staff people after the staff has collected the pertinent material. It is often hard to pinpoint the exact stage at which a decision is reached. More often than not, the decision comes about naturally during discussions, when the consensus seems to be reached among those whose judgment and opinion the executive seeks.

The stages of the decision-making process might be enumerated as follows:

1. analyzing the situation to find out if there is a problem
2. collecting facts
3. analyzing the factors of the problem
4. creating new ideas and new ways to tackle the problem
5. weighing alternative courses of action
6. deciding on a single definite course of action
7. following up.

Assisting management in all of these stages today are staff people.

According to the late Professor Sumner H. Slichter, "The enormous increase in staff means that business is far better prepared than ever before to deal with its problems, to make plans, and to develop policies—in short, to overcome difficulties and to attain its objectives." *

It is my own view that an important factor in the tremendous increase in our economy's productivity over the last fifty years has been the addition of qualified staffs to aid in the planning and decision-making process. And this is as true for government as for business. Accordingly, I will devote the greater part of my comments to the development and present use of staff organizations.

By the term "staff," I refer to those people whose job it is to investigate, analyze, recommend, interpret, and follow up on problems for the chief executive. Usually they specialize in some specific aspect of the senior executive's work, such as economic analysis or industrial relations problems. The staff member's relationship to an executive is that of working on the latter's behalf; of doing things the executive feels necessary but hasn't sufficient time for; of passing along interpretations and instructions in the name of the senior executive but not as authoritative orders from the staff person.

Management of large business organizations today requires the assistance of many staff people, specialists, and staff departments. This would be the case even if there were no external forces with which to deal.

But in this day and age, the day-to-day decisions of management are greatly influenced by factors outside its control —such as government policy in taxation, fiscal and monetary affairs, social welfare legislation, regulations affecting

* *Potentials of the American Economy, Selected Essays of Sumner H. Slichter* (J. T. Dunlop, ed.), Harvard University Press, 1961, p. 24.

government contracts, and many other public matters. An adequate staff has become even more essential if management is to keep informed about current laws and regulations and the probable future trends in legislation.

THE GROWTH OF STAFF ORGANIZATIONS

Back in 1914 when I joined Eastman Kodak, the company was considered a fairly large concern. It employed some 10,000 people both here and abroad, its products were sold throughout the world, and it had unique status in its field. Yet the principal executives had no staff assistants.

In the White House that same year, to help him reach the almost infinite decisions necessary to the running of our federal government, Woodrow Wilson had no more than five staff men.

Nowadays at Kodak there are many staff assistants, several with vice-presidential stature, and a number of separate staff departments at the executive offices.

In the White House on January 1 of this year, there were approximately 50 staff people and a total force of over 400 employees. In the entire executive offices of the President, including the six staff agencies, there was a total force of nearly 2,700.

Why did this growth of staff come about? How did business and government function without staff people? How do staffs aid in formulating policies and in reaching decisions? Have we gone too far? Is top management becoming overly dependent on staff work? These are some of the questions we shall attempt to discuss.

Military organizations have long understood the uses and value of staff. All the way from the least to the greatest units, line officers have traditionally had their staff assistants. I recall that in World War I at the headquarters staff of the general in command of a division of 28,000 men, there were four sections of staff officers—G-1 for personnel, G-2 for intelligence, G-3 for operations and training, and G-4 for supply.

It has also long been customary for the line supervisors in factories to have staff assistants, especially since the development of "scientific management" under the pioneer work of Frederick W. Taylor early in this century. But the importance of staff work at the top-management level in government and industry has been recognized only in recent decades.

Possibly one factor has been the personalities involved. Political leaders have often tended to be picturesque people with strong leadership qualities; otherwise they would not have emerged from the rank and file. Being strong individualists, they have felt the need for relatively little staff assistance. Similarly, the traditional captain of industry was a rugged individual who knew his own business better than anyone else and relied very little on others for aid in making major decisions. He operated on intuition or hunches; frequently they seemed to be *inspired* hunches.

Some of these men were geniuses. I believe George Eastman, founder of the Eastman Kodak Company, was. Yet, like other great industrialists, Mr. Eastman worked very long hours, six days a week, and in close, continuous contact with the other officers of the line command. Because the business was still relatively simple, his response to a problem on any phase of operations was usually more a matter of knowledge than of inspiration.

Like so many successful businessmen, Mr. Eastman was careful about details and abhorred waste. I recall an instance in connection with the telephone system in his large residential establishment. Because of a change in the policy of the local telephone company, he had to give up his personally owned inter-communications system and rent one from the telephone company, with a small additional charge for each phone. Before going on a hunting trip to Alaska, he gave me a list of the outlets to be installed while he was away. The number of phones was reduced but there were still about fifteen.

When the system was installed, the housekeeper called me and was quite upset because Mr. Eastman had not provided a phone in the greenhouse or in the garage. She thought this had been a mistake and wanted to know if it would be all right to have the two phones installed. Although the cost would be only nominal, Mr. Eastman had been so specific in his instructions to me about the phones he wanted that I told her I would write him about it. In about two weeks his secretary received a cable which included the following: "Tell Folsom phone for garage okay but not greenhouse." It was about that same year that Mr. Eastman announced gifts of over $15 million to certain universities!

Although Mr. Eastman had very little formal training and education, he is ranked as one of the world's great industrialists. He was an inventor, a keen businessman, an imaginative merchandiser, a tireless seeker after new ideas, and an eminent philanthropist.

Another of Mr. Eastman's remarkable qualities was the vision to see that future progress would require industrial leaders of a kind different from himself. How many men can countenance such an idea? But it was Mr. Eastman who pointed out that, while he and his contemporaries made out reasonably well, the business leader of the future would need all the education he could get. This was one of the underlying factors in the evolution from intuitive to more scientific management at the Eastman Kodak Company.

Due to the rapid progress of industry following World War I, top-management people began to realize that they needed more assistance in arriving at sound decisions. They no longer could keep in close touch with all operations, especially the new developments. Each day new problems would arise that were beyond their ken; products were becoming more technical and diversified; organizations were becoming more complex. In addition, they had to deal with many new problems outside their own business. So staff men—specialists in their fields—were gradually added to assist them.

When I first joined Kodak, I had the good fortune to be assigned as a staff man to Frank Lovejoy, then general manager of manufacturing departments and later president of the company. Mr. Lovejoy was an able executive, an inspiring leader, and a great humanitarian.

One of my first assignments was in the statistical field. (Fortunately, I had taken the first course given in business statistics at the Harvard Business School.) Characteristic of Mr. Lovejoy's concern for people, whether customers or employees, he wanted charts on (1) complaints received from customers regarding product quality and (2) the causes of labor turnover—why people left the company.

After my return from the First World War, I became a

staff assistant to Mr. Eastman, who was then president. It was about that time that he and Mr. Lovejoy realized the need for more factual information on all phases of the business, and I was asked to organize a statistical department. There were very few companies with such departments in those days.

This was typical of staff development. At first, a single staff man was added and then, after the need and work developed, a separate department was set up to serve top management as well as the principal division heads.

I shall discuss first the functions of the top-management staff and then, in Chapter 2, the functions of several staff departments as each contributes to the decision-making process. My comments will be concerned primarily with the operation of large business organizations—large enough to require staff departments as well as staff executives.

The management of a small business requires the same type of assistance, but obviously the size of the staff must be considerably less. One staff man, for example, may do the work of a department of a larger company. Often, as in the case of legal, patent, economic, or public relations advice, outside consultants may provide the service.

FUNCTIONS OF TOP-MANAGEMENT STAFF

Before discussing the major contributions that can be made by staff work, let me first reaffirm the fact that the job of establishing policies and making major decisions—in government as in business—belongs to the line organization, which for top-level matters means, of course, the chief executive. And the executive must assume full responsibility for these decisions.

There are six principal functions to be performed by the immediate staff assistants to top management:

1. to relieve the executive from routine matters which do not require his attention by making decisions on these matters in accordance with policies established by the chief executive;

2. to collect and analyze data, both from within and outside the organization, and make carefully considered recommendations regarding new ideas, plans, and the formation of policy;

3. to review and follow up major policy decisions by acting as liaison and helping the principal department heads to interpret these decisions;

4. to help coordinate the work of the various divisions and departments;

5. to follow certain aspects of the business, such as product development or pricing policies, throughout the entire organization; and

6. to undertake special assignments.

If staff people are to operate effectively, they must have full access to information. They must be given sufficient prestige and authority to go anywhere in the organization for information—as long as major decisions come through the line organization. At Kodak, as in many business firms, a number of top-management staff people are vice-presidents of the company.

The most effective number of top-management staff people depends, of course, on the nature of the organization and the personal working habits of the executive. For example, a chief executive who generally feels it necessary to delve personally into the details of a problem may not need as large a staff as an executive who examines only the salient aspects of a problem and then turns it over to his staff for study, recommendations, and follow-up. Of course, every successful executive must have the capacity to delve into details and get the essential facts when the occasion demands, as it often does.

The optimum number of staff people also depends on whether the organization operates on an easy, informal basis, with its chief executive easily accessible to the principal line officers and others who need to see him, or whether it is set up on a more bureaucratic basis, with a formal channel of staff people whom one must go through first. Most companies are now generally in the "informal" category, which is characterized also by many decisions being reached through the means of *ad hoc* conferences—special and sometimes spontaneous meetings of the principal executives concerned with the subject at hand.

Although a few large companies still seem almost as bureaucratic as some government agencies, the trend appears to be away from this practice. In fact, large government Departments can also be operated efficiently on a basis of ready access to the principal executives, with informal discussions.

The management group at Kodak operates more on the informal basis. For example, members of top management often, where expedient, contact directly someone down the line if they know that person is best informed on a particular matter. This degree of flexibility helps to make our internal communication more effective. As a result, there is no elaborate top-management staff organization at Kodak.

Rather, small groups of staff people are assigned to each of the principal operating executives.

Illustrations of the Use of Top-management Staff. It is important that at least one key staff assistant be available for special assignments and be sufficiently free from routine duties so that he can be thinking of the business as a whole —especially with respect to the need for new programs and developments, whether in products, services, or organizational matters.

As an illustration of this type of staff work, I recall an assignment given me in 1927 to study the pension problems of the Kodak company.

The background was as follows: Mr. Eastman had devised a wage dividend plan, which the company adopted in 1912. Under this plan, subject to authorization by the board of directors, a cash dividend was (and still is) paid each year to employees, with the amount based on the cash dividends declared on the common stock during the previous year and on the individual's earnings over the five years preceding the payment date.

By 1927 the wage dividend rate had reached the equivalent of six or eight weeks' pay for employees of five years' service. Each check was accompanied by a letter from Mr. Eastman to the effect that the wage dividend should not be considered as current income but used as a savings fund for old age or emergencies.

By this time the company was over forty years old. Many employees were beginning to reach retirement age and some of them were beginning to slow down. The company used the income from a welfare fund to pay a retirement bonus, but management realized that some employees would still be unable to get along if retired and naturally hesitated to lay them off.

When Mr. Eastman was first approached about a pension plan, he took the position that with the company paying at least the going rate of wages and with the substantial annual wage dividend designed to enable the individual to save for his old age, the company had done its part and it would be up to the individual to take care of his retirement himself.

One day, an insurance broker with whom Mr. Eastman was well acquainted got an appointment with him and began to discuss pensions. Mr. Eastman called me in and, probably more out of courtesy to his visitor than conviction, he asked me to investigate the whole question of pensions and find out what other companies were doing.

My investigation, which took several months, revealed that all the companies I approached realized the need for a pension plan. Some of the larger ones had such plans, but very few were on a sound actuarial basis. One of the large insurance companies had just devised a group annuity plan that seemed to be a sound financial approach. We compiled a great deal of statistical information upon which cost estimates could be based; then, after many conferences with Kodak executives, including the general counsel (T. J. Hargrave, now chairman of the board), and with the insurance company and the insurance broker, we agreed upon a group annuity plan.

We also reached the conclusion that the company would not be justified in paying the cost of a pension on top of the wage dividend. The plan we finally presented to Mr. Eastman therefore included a reduction in the cash wage dividend sufficient to pay the cost not only of the annuity plan but also of a life insurance and total disability plan. The welfare fund, together with a large tax refund which resulted from overpayment of the excess profits tax during World War I, was sufficient to finance a large portion of the high initial cost of the pension plan.

When the plan was recommended to Mr. Eastman he readily agreed. He considered an alternative aspect of the plan, which would have provided that the funds be invested by the company and not turned over to the insurance company, but it took Mr. Eastman only a couple of minutes to reach a decision. He felt that these funds for employees' annuities should be removed as far as possible from commercial hazards, that we had had no experience in the actuarial field, and that it would be safer to turn the funds over to an insurance company that was in the business. (This was before the banks and trust companies got into the investment of pension funds to any extent.)

The plan was well received by employees and has proved very successful over the years.

Nowadays, of course, an assignment such as Mr. Eastman gave me would be handled by the staff of the industrial relations department in cooperation with other staff departments. But even today there are always important new problems arising that do not necessarily fall within the province of any particular staff department. Such problems can be effectively studied by a member of top management staff who is free enough of other responsibilities to devote considerable time to the study.

In my subsequent experience at Kodak and in government, I found it very helpful to have a young staff assistant who could make special studies and investigations, obtain information directly by cutting across regular channels, and serve as a general liaison man.

Perhaps it might be helpful if I also described briefly a specific function of Kodak's general-management staff today —such as the pricing function.

Kodak officials believe the responsibility for pricing is best retained by general management because the company's pricing philosophy is closely coordinated with the over-all goals and policies of the company. The effort in pricing is to offer products whose value, in terms of quality, service, and price, will be attractive to the customer in comparison with the multitude of other products competing for his dollar . . . to reach a broad market with our products and thus gain the benefits of mass production and full employment . . . and to secure a profit that will yield a fair return on sales and invested capital.

For any given product, the sales and manufacturing executives submit price recommendations to a very small general-management staff headed by a vice-president of the company. The sales people indicate the volume of the product they think they can sell at various price levels, and the manufacturing people indicate the production cost situation at various possible production levels. For supplementary information the general-management staff calls freely upon the services of other departments, such as the market research and statistical departments. The comptroller's division does the over-all cost analysis for the product, including production, distribution, sales and advertising, research, and general administrative costs, and it also calculates the profit picture.

Thus, much of the computation and fact-gathering has been accomplished within the various staff departments, and the members of the general-management staff can concentrate on interpreting the facts, arriving at judgments regarding the optimum price, and discussing the matter with the individual manufacturing and sales executives.

The general-management staff does not arbitrarily establish prices, but tries through persuasion to bring the sales and manufacturing executives into agreement. In the rare instances where they fail to reach an agreement, the decision is worked out with the general manager of the company, who of course reviews many of the key pricing decisions.

In pricing, as in so many other aspects of the business, management must be ever mindful of its responsibility to achieve an equitable balance of the interests of consumers, dealers, shareholders, and employees—all, of course, in the light of market and competitive factors.

Before leaving the subject of top-management staff, I should like to comment on a form of staff work that has proved particularly useful in government—so-called task forces to study important problems. Task forces are composed of people who are outside the departments immediately affected. Because of their more objective viewpoints, these people are often able to make valuable suggestions. Task forces can be effectively utilized in business as well as in government.

DELEGATING AUTHORITY WITHOUT LOSING CONTROL

One of the advantages of staff work is that it can enable executives to delegate authority to people in the line organization without the danger of losing touch with what is going on. A great deal of decision making, of course, must be delegated to junior executives, and initiative must be encouraged on their part. But in the absence of proper liaison, delegation can easily reach the point where the principal executives are not being kept adequately informed of programs and operations.

Military organizations have long been aware of the need to maintain lines of communication from a platoon leader right up to the commanding general, and in the reverse order. Similarly in business, liaison work can be conducted by top-management staff working closely with the staffs and heads of the line organization. But there is not the need in business for such rigid lines of communication as are necessary in the military.

A good staff at headquarters can overcome or offset problems resulting from a decentralized organization. Without staff liaison, some divisions might begin to think too much of what is good for themselves rather than for the company as a whole. For instance, long-range research projects may be passed up because of fear of the effect on immediate profits. But a strong central staff—vested with sufficient authority and prestige, and tempered by its own good judgment and ability to work tactfully with others—can keep division management aware of over-all company policies as established by the chief executive.

Of course, there is a limit to the amount of authority that can be delegated. All major company policies should be established by the chief executive. And, in delegating liaison responsibility to his staff, it is important that the chief executive retain an effective amount of personal contact himself; else he may in time lose touch—and eventually lose control.

COORDINATING OPERATIONS

A difficult problem in present-day large organizations, with decentralized organization and much delegation of responsibilities, is the coordination of the various operations so that all departments work in unison.

An effective means for coordination can be provided by a management advisory committee consisting of the executives in charge of the principal divisions. Such a committee does not take away the decision-making function from the chief executive, as it is purely informational and advisory in nature. But it does serve as a focal point for keeping the principal executives informed on new developments and policy changes.

It provides the chief executive with an opportunity to obtain the views of all who are directly interested in a specific problem and the objective opinions of others in the organization. Such a committee also is helpful in facilitating the exchange of information, as between the sales and production managers, the research director, and other administrative and staff executives. In addition, it enables the individual members to feel out other executives on plans they have under discussion and to obtain ideas on programs being considered.

The existence of a management advisory committee does not interfere with the responsibilities of line and staff executives, as they must still deal directly with the top officers in obtaining decisions. In some respects such a committee serves the same function as the President's Cabinet in the federal government, but it can be a much more closely knit organization in a business concern.

A management advisory committee of this type, small in size and meeting weekly, was very effective at Kodak during the years just after Mr. Eastman relinquished the active management of the company. As the top organization grew, however, and the committee enlarged to include many more executives, it became more of an informational group, meeting less frequently, rather than a group to discuss major policies with a view toward helping the chief executive reach decisions. A smaller executive committee now performs some of the functions originally handled by the management advisory committee; other functions are performed by various other committees and groups set up to deal with specific fields.

Perhaps a specific example of coordination at Kodak today would be helpful. One of the key management jobs of the company is to plan, coordinate, and review continuously the company's new-product programs. This is vitally important, as a company's life blood is its never-ending procession of new products.

These new-product programs are the subject of regular meetings at which research and development projects are planned, coordinated, and reviewed—especially with an eye toward the needs and opportunities of the marketplace.

The general manager of the company and his staff meet with the director of research and the production and sales managers. The general manager's staff consists of three vice-presidents (one to coordinate manufacturing, one for product development, and one for price-profit matters) and several administrative assistants.

The meetings are attended by different operating executives, depending upon the product line under review. This provides a flexible and effective way to bring together the right executives for this key operation. Follow-up and coordination are handled by the general manager's staff, but the responsibility for action is that of the operating executives.

ROLE OF THE STAFF AS A "CHECK AND BALANCE"

The use of staff by management can be an effective tool not only in coordinating the activities of the various divisions, in liaison work, and in the follow-up of decisions, but also in the development of new programs and products. C. 1

Staff people, such as a budget officer, chief statistician, and other assistants to top management, can often keep a more objective viewpoint of the company's over-all situation than can the head of a division. It is their responsibility to see that the chief executives are given the full picture, with arguments pro and con. In this way, they serve as something of a "check and balance" for management. With adequate staff work, there is no reason for top management to make decisions that are not based on proper consideration of the pertinent facts.

One of the principal differences between management in business and in government is that business management, if it chose, could make quick and perhaps arbitrary decisions. The principal executive reports to the directors, who are concerned only with general, over-all, policy matters.

In government few, if any, major policy decisions can be made by the top executives—even the President—without full discussion by many individuals with widely different viewpoints. The ability to persuade is a most important trait. Even if the top official has the authority to make the decision, he can be called and questioned about it before and after by Congressional committees. As a result, most important matters are thoroughly discussed by people representing various interests and groups before a decision is reached. The resulting decision is presumably based on what is considered best for the country as a whole. The process is slow, but it is democratic and provides many safeguards against hasty and undue action.

Through a staff that has the respect and confidence of line executives, business management can obtain this same protection. The process, of course, does not have to be as long and drawn-out as in government, as management is dealing with a closely knit group of people, all of whom have the same basic objective.

Many executives find that as important matters are fully discussed with their immediate staff and departments heads —and assistant department heads who are probably closer to certain matters—not only will new facts be developed but the process itself will have an important effect upon the morale of the organization. Similarly, when differences of opinion exist, executives are finding it more effective to establish their point of view through persuasion rather than peremptory decisions. The ability to persuade can be as important in business as it is in government. The more people who feel they are participating in major decisions, the more effective will be the follow-through, and the easier it is to build *esprit de corps*.

Businessmen can also learn from government that while many incentives—such as salary, bonus, and stock options

—are important, they are not the only incentives which are necessary to build up a good organization. For example, many top Civil Service career men who have reached the limit of their salary range perform just as capably for the government as many men doing similar work in business for much higher salaries. These people are dedicated to public service, and recognition and appreciation of their services help to spur them on. These less tangible incentives are equally as important to people in industry. This leads to a question as to whether, in addition to financial incentives, business should not give more attention to other types of motivation in general—particularly the need to demonstrate thoroughly to organization members the useful function they are performing for society.

STAFF ORGANIZATION HAZARDS

There are several serious hazards which must be guarded against in the growth of management staff and staff departments.

One is over-staffing. It is difficult, of course, to establish effective rules of thumb regarding the optimum number of staff people for any given situation. Generally, small groups of highly qualified staff people seem to work out best.

Over-staffing can be suspected when non-pertinent information is frequently brought up, when issues often become confused, and when decisions are too often delayed—and particularly when all three symptoms exist at once. A further aspect of over-staffing is that too many opinions, once the facts are assembled, can often lead to indecisiveness on the part of the executive.

One factor leading to over-staffing may be the attempt to

fit people to an organization chart rather than fit the chart to the persons concerned. When an executive position changes hands, the new executive may need more or less staff people than his predecessor. It is foolish to fill a staff position without first questioning whether the position is still necessary or whether the position will be used in the same manner as it was previously. There are times when staff positions should be eliminated, as well as times when new ones should be created.

Another hazard arises when the executive depends too much on his staff for getting his information. When this occurs, the executive's contacts with the line departments will probably suffer, and by getting his information second-hand he will lose the opportunity to discuss matters with the department heads, who are meeting the problems every day. Furthermore, the morale of the organization is likely to suffer. On the other hand, if he listens to the discussion of all viewpoints, he will better sense the feel of the problem and be able to learn of different approaches. Without such complete background he will not be in a position to exercise sound judgment.

Still another danger is that the staff man, to save his boss time, will begin making policy decisions for him, especially if the staff man is of high rank. For the best relations between the staff and line organizations, it is particularly important that the staff man not make major decisions except in extreme cases where the executive is unavailable, and at all such times he should make it clear that he is acting *for* his boss. The executive will have to watch this situation as, without his knowledge, some staff men are apt to assume these policy-making functions.

(These remarks do not apply, of course, in those instances when an individual serves both a staff and line function, where the chief executive delegates authority to him in certain areas.)

A corollary to this situation is when staff people fail to call important issues to the attention of management because they believe the solution will cost too much to justify its acceptance, or because they think they know in advance that management would turn down their recommendation. When they do this, they are making the decisions themselves and are not giving management the opportunity to decide.

For example, suppose a company's wage administration staff people believe that the current wage incentive plan includes some provisions that run counter to the company's general wage policy. If they do not call the problem and the preferred solution to the attention of management because they believe it would cost too much to rectify past mistakes, they are in fact making the decision that no correction is possible. This, however, should be management's decision.

There is also a tendency by some staff men to shield their bosses from unpleasant news and contacts. Such protection can often go too far and prevent the executive from gaining pertinent information or learning of alternative points of view. As I pointed out earlier, the chief executive must be sure that all lines of communication are open to him.

A further hazard is that top staff people may refer matters to their boss which should first have been referred to a principal department head—who actually may have been able to make the decision.

These organizational hazards can be corrected without much difficulty, but they can creep in without top management becoming aware of them. It is unfortunate when they do creep in, because a *properly utilized* staff can be so helpful to management in arming it with the pertinent facts upon which to base sound decisions. In fact, effective staff work is one of the chief reasons why business management has become, as President Eliot suggested, a *profession* as well as an art.

2

ROLE OF STAFF UNITS IN A BUSINESS ORGANIZATION

In this chapter I shall try to be more specific in portraying some of the ways in which staff can assist top management in the process of decision making and policy forming. As illustrations, I shall describe the functions of six staff areas that have become highly important to business management —industrial research, statistical and planning, budgeting, market research, industrial relations, and executive recruitment and training.

There are, of course, other staff areas that make important contributions to top management's decisions—including legal and patent departments, comptroller's divisions, office management groups, and public relations staffs. Certain aspects of public relations will be discussed in the final chapter, but otherwise I shall not cover these staff functions in this book.

INDUSTRIAL RESEARCH

The vital function that industrial research performs in ensuring future progress of an industrial concern is now well recognized by management. I shall touch only upon its activities that may be considered staff functions for top management.

The primary purpose of industrial research and development is to ensure the present and future technological soundness of the company. Probably the most important objectives are to develop new and improved products and processes and advanced techniques of manufacture so the company can maintain a satisfactory competitive position. The research and development organization should also afford a reservoir of scientific and technical knowledge and experts and should provide technical service to other divisions of the company.

Eastman Kodak was one of the pioneer companies, along with others such as General Electric, Bell Telephone, and DuPont, to establish a comprehensive research laboratory. Kodak, as well as these other companies, set aside a certain portion of its funds from the very beginning to be devoted to *basic* research—the quest for new knowledge in the basic sciences underlying the business. This is one of the principal reasons why the research laboratories in all these companies have been so successful.

The late Dr. C. E. Kenneth Mees, who established the Kodak Research Laboratories in 1912 and so ably directed their activities for forty years, had this to say about research administration:

Research is a gamble. It cannot be conducted according to the rules of efficiency engineering. Research must be lavish of ideas, money, and time. The best advice is—don't quit easily; don't trust anyone's judgment but your own, especially don't take any advice from any commercial person or financial expert; and, finally, if you really don't know what to do, match for it.

The best person to decide what research work shall be done is the man who is doing the research. The next best is the head of the department. After that you leave the field of best persons and meet increasingly worse groups. The first of these is the research director, who is probably wrong more than half the time. Then comes a committee, which is wrong most of the time. Finally there is the committee of company vice-presidents, which is wrong all the time.

Of course, Dr. Mees said this with his tongue in his cheek —he himself was a company vice-president! As a matter of fact, Dr. Mees' department was the first at Kodak to operate on an annual budget, and this came about at his own suggestion. Yet, certain elements of truth in his statement ring through, loud and clear.

Perhaps I might best illustrate the role of the research director in assisting management's decision-making process by relating the story of how Kodachrome Film—the first commercially successful color film—came to be introduced in 1935.

From the earliest days of photography in the last century, one of the greatest goals was to achieve a system for taking pictures in color. Naturally, when the Kodak Research Laboratories were established in 1912, one of management's high-priority objectives at that time was the development of a color film. Yet, although various methods were tried

29

experimentally, a successful color process proved an elusive goal.

During the late 1920's Kodak's laboratories made important advances in basic research in the area of sensitizing dyes. These advances gave greater promise to an approach toward color photography which Dr. Mees knew was being studied independently by two young photo enthusiasts in New York City. The Kodak laboratories had been supplying them with experimentally coated plates since 1922, but the young men had been handicapped by their inadequate facilities.

Both of them—Leopold Mannes and Leopold Godowsky—were professional musicians. And although Mannes had a B.A. degree in physics from Harvard University and Godowsky had taken courses in physics and mathematics at the University of California, both considered music their foremost interest. Yet Dr. Mees was sufficiently impressed by their work in color photography research that in 1930 he induced Kodak's management to make financial agreements with them regarding their patents and to offer them positions in the Kodak Research Laboratories.

At the Kodak laboratories Mannes and Godowsky came in contact with organized groups who could carry out the technical operations required to make photographic emulsions, to synthesize the necessary chemicals, to experiment with sensitizers—and thereby attempt to realize Mannes's and Godowsky's ideas for a new process of color photography.

Their work, of course, was only one of a number of possible ways toward color photography that were under study at the laboratories.

The two musicians caused no little amount of consternation at Kodak. Word got around that they spent their evenings playing chamber music with faculty members of Rochester's Eastman School of Music. And many of their research associates did not realize that their periodic whistling of classical music in the darkroom served as an accurate darkroom timing device.

For over a year there was little concrete progress with which to impress management. Yet Dr. Mees continued to see that management provided funds for their work, as well as for the quantity of work that had to be carried on concurrently in order to make effective use of their efforts.

Early in 1933 management's patience was rewarded by Mannes's and Godowsky's development of a two-color system of color photography. While it hardly provided perfect color, it was the best process yet devised, and it *was* commercially feasible. The pressure was on to place the film on the market.

Dr. Mees, Mannes and Godowsky, and the laboratory staff, however, were convinced that a three-color system, if it could be perfected, would provide much better color. Dr. Mees, therefore, arranged to have more extensive laboratory facilities and a larger number of research personnel placed at the disposal of Mannes and Godowsky.

Dr. Mees did assent to management's decision to take initial steps toward placing the two-color film into production. But this only hastened the work of the research team, which came up with an effective three-color process before production plans on the initial film had been completed.

On April 15, 1935, a film based on the three-color process was introduced under the trademark of "Kodachrome Film."

At the formal announcement, Mannes and Godowsky played sonatas between screenings of pictures taken with the new film.

The film was an immediate success, and the quality of pictures made with it in 1935 was very nearly similar to that obtained with Kodachrome Film for over twenty-five years.

The Kodak laboratories have carried on constant development work since that time. They made over a dozen important modifications in Kodachrome Film which speeded up its processing cycle, improved aspects of its quality, and extended its range of usefulness. In addition, the company has introduced a wide variety of other color films over the years.

This story illustrates, of course, the importance of a strong program of fundamental as well as developmental research. But it also illustrates the need for a well-qualified research director who is relied upon by management for counsel regarding the direction of the company's investment in research.

The established procedure at Kodak is for management to provide funds for basic research, exploratory research, and early-stage development work without specifying in detail their allocation to the various technical programs. Since the vice-president in charge of research is a member of the management advisory committee and is continually in touch with management informally, his thinking and plans for the research and development program are conveyed to management on an uninterrupted basis. Through the same channels, the interests of management are also well known to the director and his staff. The result is that the distribution of effort between long-range and short-range technical objectives in the laboratory is reviewed and shifted smoothly.

Research and development effort is divided between the research laboratories, which operate as a staff department to general management, and the manufacturing divisions. The major responsibility of the research laboratories is to provide scientific and technical knowledge, invention, and development which is directed primarily toward what the company will be doing technologically in the next five to ten years. Thus their program is basically long-range.

The more short-range programs, oriented toward the improvement of current products, processes, and manufacturing techniques, are largely the responsibility of the manufacturing divisions. These divisions also assume most of the responsibility for the late-stage development of new products and processes and their introduction into the product line.

This arrangement gives the research laboratories maximum freedom to carry on basic and exploratory research and early-stage development. In the Kodak Research Laboratories approximately 20 percent of the effort is given to basic research, 40 percent to exploratory research and early-stage development, and 20 percent to the development of specific new products and processes. The remaining 20 percent is given to technical service both within the laboratories and to the manufacturing divisions.

For late-stage development work in the manufacturing divisions, a formal system has been established by which funds for specific objectives are reviewed and allocated by management. New-product programs are the subject of regular meetings (see pages 20 and 21) convened by the general manager of the company. At these meetings a priority of effort is established for each project, based on economic studies, the state of the art, and competition.

For example, projects are assigned a top priority, a high priority, a medium priority, or a low priority. These priorities then serve as guide lines for executives down the line in determining the amount of development effort to be expended on new products, and in preparing the budgets to finance these efforts. The more important programs which involve costly effort or new concepts or policy determination are reviewed by the company's executive committee. By this means, management has more direct control over the expenditure of money for immediate commercial objectives.

Judging by the expansion of industrial research and development over the past decade, I would expect that managements in the years ahead will allocate increasing funds for this work, and that the problems of administration will become more complex and more difficult. In particular, it appears that managements are giving greater attention to the research and development program, not only in planning the over-all objectives, but in reviewing broadly the various individual projects. There also appears to be growing interest by management in finding ways to assess the effectiveness of the research and development effort.

Of course, as Dr. Mees pointed out in his own inimitable way, it is not consistent with the spirit and method of conducting research to expect that management can have the knowledge and background to evaluate fully all research efforts. On the other hand, it is important that management understand and participate in the evaluation of technical programs when the results indicate that serious thought should be given to the commercial exploitation of the findings—when large expenditures of money are involved and when the combined efforts of manufacturing and sales are required to launch and support a new product or process.

STATISTICAL AND PLANNING

A fundamental responsibility of top management is that of forecasting and planning. Decisions in this area enable the company to adapt its operations logically and profitably to the changing business environment. And here is where staff people—by gathering and analyzing statistical data and obtaining judgments from many people throughout the company—can make one of their greatest contributions to the effectiveness of management.

Directed toward this end at Kodak is a statistical department, which was organized in 1921 with the department head reporting directly to the president.* Its prime function is to accumulate statistics regarding all phases of the business—from industrial relations to the prices of purchased goods—everything except costs and profits, which of course are the comptroller's area of responsibility.

Once a system is developed, the procedure for handling the statistics and charts on most of these business factors may be made more or less routine. But the functions which deal with forecasting business conditions and then, in turn, making projections of the company's own sales, can never become routine. These functions are probably the depart-

* The head of Kodak's statistical department today reports directly to the treasurer.

ment's most important job, as the level of sales determines the level of most other activities within a company.

Through carefully prepared sales forecasts, a good statistical staff can help management to avoid sudden changes in employment and inventories and to plan construction programs on a more evenly scheduled basis. Widespread improvement in inventory management and construction planning would help to eliminate leading causes of the recurring recessions this country has experienced since the war.

In Kodak's early years, the sale of many photographic products was highly seasonal. Long before the statistical department was organized, the plant management had devised a plan to estimate sales a year in advance and produce photographic film and paper at an even rate during the year, building up inventories during the slack season to meet the peak demands. While this involved additional expenditures for air-conditioned warehouses and additional investment in inventories, the cost was much less than would have been required to provide a plant of sufficient size to meet the peak sales load—not to mention the difficulty of hiring temporary employees.

For this reason, Kodak's staff organization gained an early start in forecasting business conditions and sales. Perhaps a brief description of the system which Kodak has developed over the past forty years would be of interest.

First, assumptions are made about the general economy. An economic section prepares the initial assumptions. Our people analyze a considerable amount of economic data and keep in touch with the views of economists in the government, universities, and other business firms. Economic forecasts for the coming year and for four additional years are worked out. These are expressed in terms of a number of economic indexes.

The data, in chart form, are presented to the management advisory committee, which consists of seventeen principal executives. After review and approval by top management, these general business assumptions are disseminated to various executive groups, planners, sales groups, and budget people throughout the company. Complete reviews of the economic forecasts are made twice a year and are supplemented by a brief verbal review of business conditions each month.

The second step is to study how the sales of each product group have usually reacted to changes in the economy. Then, in preparing the sales forecasts, projected sales trends are modified by relevant factors in the economic assumptions. Forecasts are made for both domestic sales and exports.

The sales forecasts are further modified in discussions with sales, production, and distribution executives. Adjustments are made for plans to introduce new products and for other modifying factors, such as changes in the competitive situation, price changes, the size of dealer inventories, and special sales and advertising plans.

The forecasts are finally reviewed in detail by the finished products committee under the chairmanship of the general manager of the company. This committee includes principal executives in the areas of sales, production, advertising, distribution, and production planning, as well as the treasurer, the comptroller, and the chief statistician.

Forecasting, of course, is a continuous program. Management reviews of forecasts are made every four weeks.

I should like to point out several features of Kodak's fore-casting system.

First, top management is related closely to the planning function. Its decisions are required at regularly scheduled steps in the system.

Second, economic and statistical research and sales fore-casting are a function handled objectively by people who specialize in this work.

And third, every effort is made to bring into the planning process all executives, including middle management, who are responsible for helping to adapt plans to changing economic conditions. This wide participation encourages sound planning and decision making all down the line.

In this system we can see illustrations of both the sequence of decision-making stages and the role of a staff unit in these stages. The collection of original data and the analysis of the general economic situation are done by the economic section. Then, after further consideration of the probable range of general business activity, a group of top executives approves a particular set of assumptions. At this point the executives have made a decision upon which the next decision-making process will be based.

In this next step, which is the sales forecast for each product group, the staff does further analytical work. It coordinates its efforts with sales and other line executives in arriving at estimates to be submitted to management, and it is management, of course, who approves—or decides on—the final estimates.

The decision process has been carried through mainly by the staff in the earlier stages of fact collection and analysis and the consideration of various possible decisions. Top management has entered the decision process at the later stage of choice—settling on one set of economic assumptions or approving a particular dollar-volume sales forecast for each product group.

While business forecasting is, of course, a hazardous undertaking, Kodak's experience has, on the whole, been favorable. Over the past thirty years, our January estimates of total sales for the ensuing year have been within 5 percent of actual sales in twenty of the years, and within 10 percent in all but four years—1932, 1937, 1941, and 1950.

Along with many other factors, effective forecasting has helped to bring about greater stabilization of employment. Seasonal fluctuations have been largely eliminated. Kodak's labor turnover is about one-fourth of the average in manufacturing industry nationwide. This lower turnover not only brings about lower costs through the lessened training expenses and higher productivity, but it is an important factor in achieving and maintaining high morale. In addition, stabilization of employment results in savings in the unemployment insurance tax.

Another key benefit of business forecasting is that the forward sales estimates give our manufacturing people enough advance notice of product requirements so they are able to make certain that they have the necessary buildings, machinery, equipment, and personnel to meet manufacturing schedules.

BUDGETING

The sales forecasts are a basic building block in the budgeting process.

Careful budgeting has become a fundamental means by

which management can control operations, and companies should designate a top official as budget officer. Some companies which consider the budget merely perfunctory are missing a good opportunity to improve their procedures for formulating policy and controlling operations. In recent years, the federal government budget procedure has been greatly improved. A careful study of the budgeting method used in the Executive Department would be of value to large companies who are not satisfied with their present procedures.

At Kodak we have found that a large budget staff at the executive office is not necessary, as most of the detailed work is done at the plant or division level in the accounting, statistical, and planning departments. Top management control of the budgeting procedure is through the budget officer—a vice-president and assistant to the president. The president has delegated a great deal of responsibility to him for working with the various divisions in coordinating their various budget proposals.

Each fall the president asks the management of the various plants and divisions to submit one-year and five-year budget proposals. The assumptions regarding general business conditions have already been agreed upon. Also, much of the work involved in making the one-year and five-year sales forecasts is near completion. Thus, all divisions start with the same basic figures.

At Kodak we use the term "budget" in three areas—the capital budget, the research and development budget, and the selling, advertising, distribution, and administrative budgets.

The capital budget for a given year specifies the proposed

company improvement projects and the cash to be expended. Each fall, estimates are received from the various divisions by about November 15, and summaries are prepared by the budget director. Top management discusses the projects with the managements of the several divisions, with particular attention to the large and new projects. The budget, when finally approved by management, is presented to the board of directors in December, describing major projects and also showing totals for the company as a whole. In approving the budget, the directors give consideration to the company's over-all financial picture, including the forecasts of estimated sales, earnings, retained earnings, depreciation, cash flow, and other pertinent factors related to the capital budget.

The approval of the over-all capital budget by the directors does not automatically result in approval of the individual projects for the coming year. Shortly before work starts on individual projects, a special expenditure requisition, which includes engineering estimates and return on investment, must be submitted for final management approval.

The capital budget, the research and development budget, and the administrative budget are all prepared in considerable detail for the coming year. In addition, a five-year forecast is prepared, which represents a summarization of the approved sales forecasts, the resultant gross-profit and operating-profit forecasts, and the forward estimates of the various budgets—all tied together in a five-year financial plan showing the forecasts of sales, earnings, and balance-sheet items. This financial forecast, as with all estimates involving earnings, is prepared by the comptroller's division.

41

With such a budget fairly firm for one year ahead and estimates for five years into the future, management is provided with background which can enable it to make better decisions on all aspects of the business.

This discussion helps to point up the tightly linked chain of decision making: We start with approved business assumptions, then follow with sales estimates, cost estimates, and profit estimates. Manufacturing schedules and schedules for the purchase of raw materials are established accordingly. The whole cycle must be in phase, and no exception to this procedure is allowed without the specific approval of either the president or the general manager of the company.

As a matter of interest, I might add that the budget procedures we have just discussed have been successfully introduced in the Eastman Kodak Company's associate manufacturing companies in Great Britain, Canada, Germany, France, and Australia. In countries where there are sales companies but no manufacturing operations, a more simplified form of budgeting is used. As a result, the management of the Eastman Kodak Company in Rochester each year has a complete forward picture of not only its operations in the United States, but throughout the world.

MARKET RESEARCH

Management must make many important decisions regarding the development and introduction of new products. The making of such decisions demands a thorough knowledge of the rapidly changing characteristics of the marketplace, and a strong market research staff can provide valuable information of this type.

For existing products, it can help to locate market opportunities and estimate dealer inventories. And it can help the advertising department evaluate existing and proposed advertising programs.

But probably the market research staff can be most helpful to management in reaching decisions relating to new products. Today management examines new product development from two viewpoints—technical excellence of the product, and the marketability of the product. Technical excellence is not in itself sufficient to cause business to invest in new products. There must also be a market need that can be developed through sales and advertising.

It is regarding this decision as to the marketability of a product that the market research staff can make valuable contributions. It can compile and analyze data on such questions as potential users of a product, probable size of the market, competitive factors, price levels, characteristics of an effective marketing plan, and effective channels of distribution.

For example, in 1952, before Kodak expanded its operations to include the manufacture of polyethylene plastic, it assured itself not only that it could make a good product, but that there was both an existing and growing future market for the product.

A market study outlined the currently known uses for polyethylene. It showed the past history of sales by end use, and through the combination of statistical projections and contacts with consumers, it provided management with an estimate of future sales potential for the industry. These projections were made with different price assumptions, since price appeared to be important in determining the

43

extent to which polyethylene would compete with other materials.

The projection using the lowest price assumption showed the following growth:

Year	Millions of Pounds
1948	18
1950	50
1952	105
Est. 1954	220
Est. 1960	500

This, as it turned out, proved to be conservative—which is the direction in which our market research people prefer to err.

Data on the production capacity and quality of product of producers already in the market were also obtained as a guide in estimating the probable share of the market that Kodak could obtain initially. In addition, a thorough examination was made of existing selling methods and the services required by users. From this data, recommendations were made as to the requirements for an effective marketing organization.

Product improvement, which requires data on consumer needs and desires, is another area in which the market research staff can effectively augment the information collected by the line organization.

INDUSTRIAL RELATIONS

One of the most important responsibilities of a chief executive is to develop and maintain the morale of the whole organization.

Good employee relations do not develop overnight; nor

can they be built by one man or several. Employee benefit plans play an important part in attracting and holding good people in an organization and in maintaining morale. These alone, however, are not sufficient unless management has the right attitude and unless the right spirit is reflected throughout the organization.

Almost every large company has a written industrial relations policy. Usually it makes good reading. Usually, too, one company's policy sounds very much like another's—for the simple reason that the over-all stated objectives do not vary greatly.

The difference shows up, of course, in the basic intent behind the written policy, and the spirit in which top management follows through. If top-management people have sincere concern and respect for employees as individuals, their attitudes will be reflected in the way their policies are carried out all the way down the line.

A good industrial relations staff can assist a great deal in initiating, coordinating, and following up these policies. This staff should keep management closely and fully informed on all matters affecting the welfare of employees and should work up policy suggestions for management approval. Members of the staff should have ready access to top management and should develop a sensitive understanding of management's intentions. For it is their staff function to coordinate with the plants and ensure the proper interpretation of policies at that level.

Another important aspect of industrial relations staff work is that of assuring comparable treatment of employees at each of the company's plants, especially in those companies which have highly diversified operations.

The scope of Kodak's industrial relations department includes such areas as employee benefits, wage and salary administration, medical services, the company newspaper, and employee training. All of these functions are of common concern to industrial relations departments, both at headquarters and in the plants. Before any new policy is recommended to management, the plant staffs participate fully in discussions, as they must follow through on the decisions at the plant level.

One of the most important functions of the industrial relations staff is to develop and carry out a sound training program for supervisors. It is vital that supervisors have a clear understanding of proper management techniques and the company's over-all policies if they are to carry out their jobs competently. In turn, the training of one's subordinates is the individual responsibility of all supervisors, from the chief executive down through those in both line and staff departments. It is a responsibility that cannot be passed on to anyone else.

The industrial relations staff should keep close watch on the labor turnover index. A high labor turnover increases costs in many ways, as discussed earlier. If a detailed analysis is made of the causes of turnover and comparisons are obtained in different plants and companies, courses of action can usually be found to correct high-turnover situations.

The industrial relations department should keep management informed on any developments which might have a bearing on the company's employee relations, such as local and national wage changes, new or modified benefit plans, government actions, work situations that are or appear to be out of tune with management's objectives, and the attitude of company people toward policies and procedures.

In keeping abreast of these problems, industrial relations people consult with colleagues in other industries; they read the literature of their vocation; and they study the situation at first hand.

Should retirement be compulsory? Should a company adopt an unemployment benefit plan to supplement the state system? What is a company's responsibility in health insurance, including major medical coverage, for both active and retired employees? How can people displaced by technological development be re-trained for new work?

These are among the more pressing questions industrial relations people are studying today. The information they come up with regarding how various plans might help employees . . . how they might affect company operations . . . and how they might be related to outside influences such as existing or pending government legislation will be of great importance in helping management to plan ahead. With such assistance, management can take steps to avoid problems before they arise.

EXECUTIVE RECRUITMENT AND TRAINING

The future of any company depends, of course, on how effectively it recruits well-qualified young people, fits them into the organization, and helps them develop to their highest potential. This is one of the most important responsibilities of top management.

It is essential to have a high-grade but small staff of men —under a director reporting to top management—to handle recruitment, placement, and follow-up for the entire organization. This staff should keep management informed about the company's ability to attract and hold highly qualified college graduates.

Won't management have to devote more thought to the problem of motivating and maintaining the morale of its highly trained college graduates? Shouldn't top management, through the company's hiring practices, encourage young people to place greater emphasis on a broad, liberal education? Shouldn't more attention be given to the continuing education of the company's executives?

These policy questions, as well as those which I have mentioned about industrial relations, illustrate a vital aspect of policy formation which is all too often overlooked—that of maintaining a continuous examination of the entire social and political scene so that problems can be recognized in their formative stage. Changing events should be observed and analyzed for their implications. With this kind of systematic survey there is a greater opportunity to make orderly decisions or choices among suitable alternatives. Without it, an organization is likely to be more often reacting to crises.

In terms of the decision-making process, I should call this kind of work the first step—analysis of the situation to find out whether a problem exists. It is the kind of work for which staff is particularly useful. Responsibility at this stage rests upon the staff to bring its analysis or concern to the attention of the chief executive.

As to the philosophy of executive recruitment and training, there is just one question on which I should like to comment briefly—the need for executives to have a broad, liberal education.

There is, at times today, a tendency to think too much

in terms of specialists in business. Certainly it is true that the staff functions we have discussed in this chapter all provide specialists in various aspects of the business to help complement the knowledge and abilities of the chief executive. Yet, with all of this assistance, what a broad range of understanding and intellectual capacity an executive must have in order to do an effective job!

To rephrase a statement * by Alfred North Whitehead, a chief executive should possess the abstract ability to break down a complex matter and then imaginatively reconstruct it . . . the capacity to visualize the reaction of a large organization to any change in one of its elements. He should have a sympathetic understanding of human nature and the conditions which evoke loyalty and participation. He should have a strong grasp of economics, not only in its generalities, but also in terms of the particular circumstances of a specific business. He should be familiar with social trends in the nation and his local community. His knowledge of the sciences should enable him to comprehend the implications of technological advances, both those already achieved and those which may yet be uncovered. His background in history and political science should enable him to foresee the reactions of government bodies to the changing times. He should be skillful in the techniques of communications, with emphasis on the art of listening and reading as well as speaking and writing. He should have the unusually keen alertness and perception that might be described as "cat's whiskers" (to borrow a phrase from Dr. Albert K. Chapman, Kodak vice-chairman). And he should

* A. N. Whitehead, *The Aims of Education & Other Essays*, The Macmillan Company, New York, 1929, pp. 141–142.

have that enlightened leadership quality which enables him to reach a decision, not out of arbitrary authority, but with the firmness that results from careful evaluation of the relevant alternatives.

In many cases, of course, an executive is hard put to know what *is* the best decision. While no one can ever be sure he has *all* the facts, there are times when the total sum of available information is really quite limited, yet the executive cannot delay his decision for further investigation. At these times especially, the soundness of the executive's reasoned guess depends to a large extent on the breadth of his education and experience.

In short, the chief executive of a large organization must be an unusually well-educated man, in both the formal and informal senses of the term. No matter how outstanding he may have been in any previous field of specialization—nor how outstanding a staff organization he may have—an executive can offer no substitute for a broad, liberal education, begun with enthusiasm in his college years and continued undiminished throughout his life.

We are fortunate to have many broadly educated men among our business leaders today, but we are in need of a larger number of liberally educated young people from whom we can draw our industrial and business leaders of tomorrow.

3

POLICY FORMATION IN THE EXECUTIVE
BRANCH OF THE FEDERAL GOVERNMENT

The process of policy formation and decision making in the federal government is a highly complex matter. During the past fifty years there have been many changes in this process, just as in decision making in industry. This is not surprising when you consider that the total federal budget expenditures in the fiscal year of 1914 amounted to less than three-quarters of a billion dollars, compared with about $81 billion in the fiscal year 1961. The number of employees in the Executive Departments of the federal government in 1914 was 400,000; by the beginning of 1961 there were 2,300,000 employees in the ten Cabinet Departments and the fifty-five independent agencies.

STAFF ORGANIZATION UNDER RECENT
UNITED STATES PRESIDENTS

Decisions of the President of the United States involve every aspect of our national life and our relations with other nations throughout the world. The President's ability to lead the nation successfully depends upon both his Administration's development of sound programs and his personal ability to convince Congress and the nation of their soundness.

The office of the President of the United States is unique and it is interesting to note how widely the various Presidents have differed in their organization and use of staff. Among the determining factors have been the President's own personality and work habits, his previous experience, the world situation, and the status of the economy. Naturally, the office has grown in size due to the increase in number and complexity of problems being faced.

In the early days, the White House staff was quite limited and the President formed his policies and reached his decisions after consulting directly with his Department heads, the legislative and political leaders, and a few close advisers.

For example, Theodore Roosevelt, with his extremely wide interest in almost every activity of government, probably took a personal hand in more activities than any other President. In this respect, he was much like his contemporary business executives.

T. R. had only one real staff man—William Loeb, Jr., a remarkable man who handled almost everything in the White House. As Louis W. Koenig described in his interesting book, *The Invisible Presidency*, Loeb also advised the President on family, personal, and social affairs. He was called "the perfect stenographer." T.R. kept three stenographers busy at once; by using uniform shorthand notes, two stenographers could be typing while the third was taking dictation. At the end of the day, having exhausted the stenographers, the President would dictate confidential letters and memorandums to Loeb.*

The size of the staff changed very little during the next twenty years. For instance, during the Wilson Administration the President's secretary and principal assistant, Joseph Tumulty, was responsible for appointments, press relations, and political and administrative details.

President Harding increased the staff and for the first time it became specialized, with a secretary to the President, an appointment secretary, a press secretary, and another assigned to political and personnel duties. The most important change brought about during President Harding's Administration—and the one which has had the most lasting effect on government—was the establishment of the Budget Bureau in the Treasury. Later it became a separate agency within the White House, the first such agency. There was very little organized work carried on in developing programs and policies until the Budget Bureau was set up. One of its functions from the beginning was to assist in developing programs and following up on decisions.

President Franklin Roosevelt greatly enlarged the staff, obtaining authority to have six administrative assistants in addition to the three Presidential secretaries. His concept was to have the White House staff small, personal, and non-specialized. There was no special staff for developing programs; President Roosevelt depended primarily on his "Brain Trust" and the Departments for this. He had wide

* Louis W. Koenig, *The Invisible Presidency*, Holt, Rinehart and Winston, Inc., 1960.

personal contacts with Senators and Congressmen, political advisers, and many persons outside the government.

During World War II a number of changes naturally were made, particularly in the use of special assistants and the addition of a Special Counsel to the President. Altogether, President Roosevelt had about fifteen staff people working directly with him, without any clear-cut lines of responsibility. In addition, he often used the sub-Cabinet personnel to handle special assignments.

To quote from Laurin L. Henry's book *Presidential Transitions:* *

Such administrative methods broke many of the managerial rules, permitted confusion, and were undoubtedly trying . . . to Roosevelt associates. But they produced a government of vigor in an unusually critical time, and they preserved the effective power of decision in the President himself.

When President Truman came to office he sought to return to the 1939 pattern. At first he had the three regular secretaries and three or four administrative assistants. He soon found it necessary to increase the staff and he reactivated the position of Special Counsel to assist in the preparation of papers and messages to Congress. He also appointed an Assistant to the President, who covered a wide range of matters but did not head up the staff. He served as a general staff man to iron out differences and coordinate activities. President Truman, in the process of obtaining facts and considering courses of action, dealt directly with his chief staff members, the Department and agency heads,

* Laurin L. Henry, *Presidential Transitions*, The Brookings Institution, Washington, D.C., 1960.

and the legislative leaders. He held almost daily meetings with his key staff men. Also, like President Franklin Roosevelt, he had wide contacts with Senators and Congressmen, both in conferences and by phone.

Some of the functions which had been centered in the White House during the Roosevelt Administration were transferred to separate agencies within the Executive Office of the President but outside the White House proper. These included the Council of Economic Advisers and the National Security Council.

The White House organization was quite different under the Eisenhower Administration. Because of President Eisenhower's long experience in military organizations he was accustomed to and appreciated the value of good staff work.

The Assistant to the President became the chief of staff, with most of the staff members reporting to the President through him. He convened and presided at White House staff conferences and worked closely with the Secretaries and agency heads. Many matters were settled by conference, without bothering the President, although the Secretary could, of course, always see the President when he or the staff felt it was necessary.

The Presidential-Congressional relations were put on a more formal basis, with regular meetings and agenda, and special staff men to deal with the legislation.

There were two or three general staff men and also a number of special assistants for functions such as national security affairs, economic affairs, public works planning, science and technology, and personnel. These special assistants did not formulate or execute policies; rather, their function was to see that the pertinent facts for sound decisions were presented to the President, and that people of varying viewpoints had an opportunity to see him. Thus, programs presented by the regular Departments or staff agencies were often reviewed by these special assistants before being presented to President Eisenhower for final action. The organization was larger and was run on a more formal basis than in previous Administrations.

In the use of the check-and-balance system of the special staffs, the President insisted that the staff agencies should stay out of operations. In later years of the Administration this policy was not always followed, especially in the case of the Budget Bureau.

President Eisenhower expected each Secretary to suggest new programs or changes in existing programs in his field. The Secretary, of course, would confer with the White House staff and sometimes the President himself before much work was done on a program to see if it would fit in with the over-all Administration policy.

Before seeing the President for a final decision on a program, the Secretary would generally discuss all angles of the problem and alternate courses of action with the White House staff. In meeting with the President to obtain the decision, the Secretary was usually accompanied by one or two of his own staff and the White House staff man, and often by the Assistant to the President. If the President raised questions or doubts about features in the proposals, further study would be required before a final decision was reached.

President Kennedy at first reduced the size of the White House staff, especially the number of assistants for special functions, such as for economic affairs. He later added some, however, and the size of the staff is now about the same as before.

Mr. Kennedy deals directly with the staff members and has not filled the position of Assistant to the President. Instead he has designated one assistant through whom domestic matters will be cleared and another through whom national security matters will go. His organization is on the informal basis of the Roosevelt and Truman Administrations. Undoubtedly further changes will be made as his Administration progresses, and probably more definite lines of authority will be established. With the growth in the size of the staff and the number of staff agencies, the loose, informal arrangement that President Franklin Roosevelt used will no longer suffice.

Thus, we have seen that the type of organization used by each President has varied. In the case of the last four Presidents, the variation has been due primarily to the personal work habits of the Chief Executive and to the increasing complexity of the problems faced.

ROLE OF THE WHITE HOUSE STAFF

There are certain functions performed by the top staff assistants which are quite similar to those performed by top staff people in industry—to relieve the President of routine matters, to arrange appointments, to act as liaison with the Departments in the interpretation of policies and decisions, to coordinate the work of the various agencies, and to undertake special assignments. In addition, top staff men of the White House serve as liaison with the Congressmen and Senators.

In the decision-making process, the staff is responsible to

see that the pertinent facts are presented, along with recommendations of the Department concerned. The staff should also see that the President is given full opportunity to consider alternate courses of action and, when necessary, the staff should suggest and develop such courses. In some cases, the staff should suggest persons inside and outside the government who should be consulted in connection with the different approaches. As in business, an important function of top staff is to suggest new ideas and plans, but it should take care not to interfere with the functions of the Department or agency affected.

Probably the most important assistance the top staff can render the President is to anticipate problems and see that preparations are made to meet them before they develop into crises in which only emergency action can be taken. This, of course, is one of the chief responsibilities of a Secretary or agency head, but the White House is the one agency concerned with the country as a whole and must at all times keep in mind the objective of what is good for the country as a whole. The individual Department may be too close to the situation to maintain as clear and objective a perspective.

An able press secretary performs a particularly important function in advising the President and handling relations with the press and other media.

The Council of Economic Advisers is very helpful to the President in the formulation of major economic policies. It also helps to coordinate economic policies throughout the Administration, prepares the annual Economic Report to the President, and assists with other messages relating to economic matters. The chief executives of many business

58

concerns, in the use of their own economic staff men, might well note how often the President consults with the chairman of the Council of Economic Advisers in the formulation of economic policies and how he uses the council in coordinating these policies.

In carrying out the council's functions during the Eisenhower Administration, the chairman met frequently with the President, attended Cabinet meetings (making periodic reports regarding the economic situation), and worked closely with the Secretaries and agency heads in developing programs affecting economic policy.

An Advisory Board for Economic Growth and Stability, consisting of the Under Secretaries of the principal Departments, met weekly with the members of the Council of Economic Advisers and served as a means of coordinating economic policy throughout the Executive Departments. This group, for instance, would go over with the council the principal recommendations to be contained in the annual economic report of the President to Congress. The members would bring up specific programs for discussion and advice. As an illustration, when I was Under Secretary of the Treasury I found the discussions with this board and the council very helpful in reaching decisions regarding the principal tax proposals the Treasury was considering in 1954.

The Budget Bureau, with its annual budget procedure, provides the President with an effective mechanism for planning . . . for coordinating and controlling the various programs of the individual Departments and the Administration's fiscal and monetary policies . . . and for management control of governmental operations. The extent to which this procedure is effective depends upon the ability and imagination of the bureau director and the interest and inclination of the President.

The Budget Bureau also reviews legislative proposals before they are submitted to Congress by the agencies and obtains views of other agencies on the proposals. In case of differences or conflicts with the Administration policies, the Budget Bureau and the White House staff will attempt to reconcile the position.

There is a great need for long-range budget planning, as so many legislative acts set up programs which run for many years and often involve an accelerating rate of expenditures. The Budget Bureau made a start in January 1961 by preparing a ten-year projection of federal budget expenditures and is now working on a program for an annual four-year expenditure projection by Departments and agencies.

The extent to which a President delegates the initiation of programs and policies to the Department and agency heads varies with different Presidents and with different Departments of the same Administration—depending upon the interests and inclination of the Chief Executive and also upon the initiative of the Secretary. If programs are initiated in the White House, larger staffs are naturally required there.

Liaison work and the coordination of activities of the various agencies and Departments are among the principal functions of the White House staff. *Ad hoc* committees, composed of staff men and Department and agency heads particularly concerned with a problem, are also useful in recommending and coordinating policies.

Most Presidents have also appointed advisory councils—

with membership from outside the government—to investigate important issues. These councils require only a small staff, as most of the staff work is done by the agency concerned. During the Eisenhower Administration, for example, several such councils worked in the defense area.

USE OF THE CABINET

Cabinet meetings can be useful in bringing about co-ordination at the top level in the Executive branch of the government. Just as the organization within the White House depends to a large extent upon the personality and working habits of the President and the times, so does his use of the Cabinet.

Woodrow Wilson, in the first part of his Administration, used the Cabinet meetings for candid discussions of policy on many important issues. Then he realized that the substance of the conferences was being leaked to the press. As a result, he gradually took up less and less at the Cabinet meetings, and the Cabinet's influence as a policy-making body declined. It met less frequently and discussed matters of less importance. Decisions were arrived at either by conferences between the President and the Cabinet member or agency head, or by correspondence.

President Harding wanted to get a group of the best minds in the Cabinet, which he intended to use as a "Council of Wise Men" who could agree upon policies. He brought in the Vice-President to sit with the Cabinet. But he too found that things began to leak, and because of this and the scandal which developed later, free discussion soon became difficult. The Cabinet meetings became short and not very important, and the President dealt directly with the Secretaries.

President Franklin Roosevelt was less optimistic than most of his predecessors concerning the potentialities of the Cabinet as a policy-making and coordinating institution. At first, his Cabinet met twice a week to discuss matters of common concern, but most of the Administration policies were worked out by Department heads in discussion with the President, by *ad hoc* groups, or by his "Brain Trust." Thus, the Cabinet meetings declined into a means of exchanging views or smoothing out Departmental conflicts.

President Truman held more frequent meetings of the Cabinet and the discussions were on a more systematic basis. He used the meetings to obtain the views of the Cabinet members on broad policy matters. The meetings were informal; there was no agenda, and no record was kept of the discussions.

President Eisenhower used the Cabinet as an important agency in policy making. He was the first President to appoint a Cabinet Secretary. Agenda were prepared in advance, accompanied by discussion papers prepared by the Department concerned. Records were kept of decisions, and the Cabinet Secretary's staff followed up on action taken by the Departments. President Eisenhower also brought into the meetings the Vice-President, the Ambassador to the United Nations, the Director of the Budget, and the Defense Mobilization Administrator. Also attending the Cabinet meetings, but not as members, were the heads of several other executive agencies and the principal staff members.

Under President Truman two staff members attended the Cabinet meetings; under President Eisenhower fifteen staff members normally attended, with the Assistant to the President and his chief deputy sitting at the Cabinet table.

President Eisenhower used the meetings to inform members of principal developments and plans, to obtain their views and to express his views on subjects for the benefit not only of Cabinet members but of the staff as well. Seldom was major action taken without the Cabinet being informed. Regular meeting dates were set for Friday morning each week. President Eisenhower had two general rules of procedure—each meeting was opened with a few moments of silent prayer and each Cabinet member's seat had to be occupied. If the Secretary was not in town, the Under Secretary would attend; or if both were away, the Assistant Secretary.

Because of the large number in the room, with the nonmembers frequently outnumbering the members, discussion generally was not as free and frank as it would otherwise have been. The result of this situation was that the Department head, as in previous Administrations, would often hesitate to put up a specific proposal to the Cabinet for discussion. He would prefer to deal directly with the President, after having first discussed the program with the White House staff members who were directly concerned. Occasionally executive sessions were held, with only the Cabinet members present, and discussions were more fruitful.

Oftentimes, when a program of general interest was being drafted, it was quite helpful to a Secretary to discuss various aspects at the Cabinet meeting and to obtain the members' views before arriving at definite conclusions.

When the first Secretary of Health, Education, and Welfare—Mrs. Oveta Culp Hobby—in 1954 prepared a broad program to extend the coverage and liberalize the various features of the Social Security Act, she and her Assistant Secretary presented the proposals to the Cabinet, using a well-prepared set of charts. They explained the existing provisions and the need for change to bring the program in line with current conditions, and then discussed each proposal in detail. There was a favorable reaction from the Cabinet members, and the President later gave his approval to the proposals. The program was presented to Congress and later enacted into law, resulting in a marked improvement in this important system. This action was particularly significant in that it definitely put the Administration and the Republican Party on record as favoring the principles underlying the Social Security System.

The Cabinet meeting is also a valuable mechanism for discussing and arriving at over-all conclusions on matters which affect all Departments, particularly in the personnel field.

Since the development of the National Security Council, matters relating to foreign affairs and national security are discussed in this council rather than in the Cabinet, which concerns itself primarily with domestic matters. In the Eisenhower Administration, procedures in the Security Council were similar in several respects to those in the Cabinet.

It is interesting to note that President Kennedy has indicated that he prefers constant contact with Cabinet members and other agency heads and that he expects to have fewer formal Cabinet meetings. He will probably find, however, that general discussions by the entire Cabinet of broad over-all policies affecting the whole country will be very helpful.

A CABINET SECRETARY'S RESPONSIBILITIES

The Secretary of a Department has four principal responsibilities:

First, as a member of the President's Cabinet he participates to varying degrees in the formation of the Administration's policies.

Second, he is responsible for the administration of his Department's programs, reporting directly to the President.

Third, he must originate new programs or changes in programs, giving careful consideration to suggestions made by his own Department, the White House, members of Congress, and the general public.

Finally, he must "sell" his program to the President, Congress, and the public.

In many respects, a Secretary's decision-making process is similar to that of a chief executive in a business concern. But there is a big difference in putting the decision into effect. In business, the line and staff organization is set to carry out the decision. In government, however, many persons have to be persuaded. A thorough knowledge of the subject, perseverance, and a power of persuasion are essential attributes of a top government official.

A Secretary must first convince the President that his program is worthwhile for the country and that the cost is justified. With the help of the President and the White House staff he must try to convince the Party leaders of the need for the program. After having a proposed bill prepared, he should help to draft the President's message presenting the proposal to Congress. He must then support the proposal at the Congressional hearings and keep in close touch with amendments. Finally, he must recommend to the President whether or not he should sign the final bill.

A Secretary naturally has to do much of his work within the public eye. It is this aspect which is often so frustrating and difficult for the businessman not accustomed to public office. A well-trained staff man to assist in relations with the press is essential, both for his advice and counsel and for carrying out the public relations functions.

In addition to periodic press conferences, it is well for the Secretary to develop personal relations with the key reporters, commentators, and columnists, especially those particularly interested in his Department. This will help the Secretary to get his proposals and views before the public. He may also find that he can obtain valuable suggestions and viewpoints from the members of the press who are in close contact with Congress and the general public. This is particularly true in such sensitive programs as those in the area of health, education, and welfare.

As to administration, the Secretary selects, with the approval of the President, his immediate assistants. He must find capable assistants, both line and staff, to whom he can delegate responsibilities. He will find that the top Civil Service people are generally competent in handling the detailed administration. In fact, a Department can generally run very smoothly without much effort on the part of the Secretary.

However, if a Secretary wants to accomplish something during his tenure, he should spend a great deal of time developing new programs as well as needed changes in existing programs. He should also be alert to the possible discontinuance of programs no longer needed. An able Secretary can provide effective leadership for his Department and can exert great influence in selling programs to the Administration, Congress, and the general public.

As to the fact-finding aspects of decision making, the Secretary depends upon the research staff of the interested agency in his Department, and upon his own analysis staff and assistants, outside interested groups, and special consultants. When it comes to new programs, the Department needs a great deal of information from outside the government. Fortunately, much of it comes in unsolicited.

Special consultant groups from outside the government have often been found very helpful, both in formulating programs and in improving administration. Two examples in my service were a special group of consultants to study the whole field of medical research and education, and consultants on administration of the Social Security System. It was encouraging to find the ready response of able people to accept these assignments.

With the scrutiny given to a Secretary's proposals by the Budget Bureau, the White House, Congressional committees, and people outside the government, there is little danger that the pertinent facts will not be brought out. The more common danger is that the process will be too long and drawn-out and that no action will be taken.

The Secretary also has full opportunity to consider several courses of action during the development of a program —because of either the emergence of new facts or the need to compromise in order to get satisfactory action.

Liaison by his staff with the staffs of the White House, Congress, and other agencies is especially important. However, with regard to Congressmen, Senators, and other top officials, it is usually important for the Secretary to make the contacts himself rather than to deal through the staffs.

With the enormous increase in the size and complexity of the federal government, the opportunity for flexibility in breaking through the regular channels and obtaining quick action is much more limited than in large business organizations. This, of course, is one of the handicaps of any large organization. There is still opportunity for speed in government, however, as illustrated by the enactment of the government employee group life insurance program in 1954.

Case Study—Government Employee Group Life Insurance Program of 1954. Because of my previous experience in employee benefit plans, I was asked to represent the Treasury on a Cabinet committee to determine how employee benefits of government employees compared with those provided by progressive industrial concerns. It was quickly apparent from an analysis I prepared that, while in several respects the government program was comparable to current practice in industry, there were two important gaps—the lack of group life insurance and group health insurance. The committee saw no reason why these two benefits should not be provided and the Under Secretary of Health, Education, and Welfare, Nelson Rockefeller, was asked to prepare suggestions for health insurance and I was asked to study proposals for group life insurance.

Working with the top staff of the Civil Service Administration and a competent authority from the insurance world, we soon prepared a plan, similar to that in common practice in industry, which would provide life insurance of one year's salary on a contributory basis. Government employees would pay the rate generally contributed by the employees in industry and the government would pay the difference. The plan would cover all employees in the executive, legislative, and judicial branches.

I submitted the proposal, with the estimates of cost, to the Cabinet subcommittee and, after gaining its approval, submitted it to the full Cabinet. I told the President and the Cabinet that I had not yet discussed the program with the insurance companies but that I felt we could obtain a satisfactory contract from them with a very low expense ratio and without commissions, as there was no selling expense involved. The President and the Cabinet gave the program general approval.

I then asked a number of life insurance presidents, representing the two associations—both large and small companies—to come to Washington to discuss the proposal. They naturally were interested and assured me that they could handle the plan at very low cost. They were hesitant about the no-commission aspect, as they did not know what the attitude of the underwriters association would be. This association, however, later agreed to this policy.

We pointed out that all the companies which were writing group life insurance should participate—to which the companies readily agreed. Later, in working out the allocations, we reduced substantially the proportion going to the largest companies so that the small companies received a proportionately greater percentage of the total than the amount of their group life insurance would entitle them to. The insurance companies agreed that it should be administered by one company as agent for the whole group.

When the details of the plan had been perfected and the estimates made of the cost, I presented the proposal to the

President and the Cabinet for their final okay. We had the Civil Service Commissioners approve the draft bill and the President sent a message to Congress endorsing the program.

As this was an extracurricular activity for me in the Treasury, I had assumed that the White House and the Civil Service Administration would carry the ball from that time on. However, they were both engaged in long drawn-out discussions on salary schedules with the same Senate and House committees that would handle the bills, and they asked me to take up the matter myself.

I immediately got in touch with the two committee chairmen. They expressed general sympathy with the proposal but expressed doubt as to whether action could be taken during that session of Congress in view of the late date— the President's message was delivered on May 19—and because of the pressure of other matters already before the committees. I pointed out that the details of the plan had been pretty well worked out, that I felt it would not take long study on the part of the committee, and that action at this session was urgent in order not to deprive employees' families of this protection. Each chairman agreed to have me appear before his committee at an early date.

The hearings were held in early June. One of a number of questions that came up was why the government did not self-insure this plan rather than take it out with private insurance companies. I had anticipated this question and pointed out that since this was a contributory plan, with employees paying more than half the cost, the government would be actually competing with the insurance industry if the government carried the risk, and that it was the policy of the Eisenhower Administration to reduce the competition between government and industry rather than to increase it. This seemed to be a satisfactory answer.

In my statement I indicated that 1,750,000 employees would be covered with insurance of about $7 billion, and that the annual cost to the government would be $22,-750,000.

In my closing statements to the committees, I urged early enactment at that session of Congress, stating that on the average about 1,000 federal employees died each month and if the enactment was delayed until the next session of Congress many families would lose the insurance benefits which this plan would provide.

The Civil Service official (Warren B. Irons, now Executive Director) and I kept in close touch with the committee and its staff after the hearings and the bill was favorably reported by the Senate committee on June 28. It passed the Senate on July 8. The Senate bill was reported out favorably by the House committee on July 30 and passed the House on August 3. The President signed the bill on August 17. An announcement was immediately made to the employees, urging them to give serious consideration to this new program.

Although we had told the Congressional committees that it would probably take two or three months to put the plan into effect, the Civil Service Administration and the insurance company decided that the plan could be put into effect much earlier. The act provided that after all employees were notified, everyone would be covered unless they signed a statement, made available to them, that they did not want to be covered. Each employee was also given the privilege of dropping out later if he did not want to continue the coverage. The plan thus became effective for all groups by September 1 at the latest.

The plan was enthusiastically received by the employees and all but about 5 percent came in immediately. The officials of the insurance company were surprised with the speed at which the plan was placed in effect. They also said that in their wide experience with many large companies initiating group life insurance programs, they could think of no organization which had handled the plan more efficiently and expeditiously than the Civil Service Administration.

This plan has now been in effect for almost seven years. On June 30, 1961, 2,325,000 employees were covered, with a total life insurance in force of $14 billion. Over 200 companies participated in underwriting the group insurance. A contingency reserve of $100 million has been accumulated and any excess of premiums over expenses beyond this reserve is returned to the government. In presenting this program to the Congressional committees, I stated that the administrative expenses and risk charges were estimated to be less than 2 percent of the premiums. The actual expenses have been well below this level.

The conclusion from this case study is that Congress and the Executive Department can cooperate effectively in inaugurating sound programs—and can do so with considerable speed when the legislation is urgent enough.

Case Study—Social and Education Research Programs. Often, however, it takes much longer to have a new program approved by Congress and, of course, proposals are frequently turned down completely.

Soon after I became Secretary I was convinced that it would be a good long-term investment if the federal government inaugurated modest programs of research in the field of education to develop better methods; of demonstration projects in welfare to show how people on relief can be restored to self-support; and of study in the area of juvenile delinquency to determine the causes and suggest methods of reducing the problem. Very little research work is being carried on in these fields and yet all levels of government are spending huge sums in these areas.

The first year I was able to obtain approval for a small program of research in both education and welfare. The next step was to get an appropriation of funds. I obtained a small grant for a cooperative educational program, but the appropriations committee earmarked more than half of the fund for work in the field of the mentally retarded. The second year we were given more leeway. During my whole term as Secretary, however, I was unable to obtain an appropriation for the welfare project, designed mainly to set up demonstration units. The Department finally obtained a small grant in 1960.

Neither I nor my successor was able to obtain action in the field of juvenile delinquency, as this was not widely viewed as a matter for the federal government to deal with. Due in part, however, to the spade work which we had done and to the increasing incidence of juvenile delinquency, Congress appropriated money for this study in 1961.

Of course, the government is not alone in regard to such delays; it often takes a long time to get action in business as well. I recall that it took us several years at Kodak, after we obtained the general management's approval, to get the advertising and the sales departments to go along with the establishment of a market research department. Now the department gets more requests for studies than its budget will permit.

MAINTAINING CONTROL IN THE EXECUTIVE BRANCH

One of the most serious management problems in the executive branch of the federal government is the result of its extent and complexity—the ten major Departments and fifty-five independent agencies. It is almost impossible for the President—whoever he may be—to maintain proper control and coordination of such a wide number and variety of agencies.

Several commissions, including particularly the Hoover Commissions, have recommended consolidation of many of these agencies into regular Departments. Some progress has been made in recent years but much remains to be done. There is a question as to whether the number of major Departments reporting directly to the President should be greatly increased, but many of the agencies could be brought into existing Departments.

One effective mechanism available to the President and Department heads for coordinating programs and controlling expenditures is the budget procedure. As a matter of fact, the budget process in the government, as far as the Executive Departments are concerned, is a more thorough process than is generally found in business.

The great weakness in the present budget system, however, is that when the President's budget reaches Congress, separate appropriations are enacted for each Department. Congress does not approve a consolidated budget, with consolidated receipts and expenditures, as does the President for his budget recommendations. The result is that until the last appropriation has been approved—generally several weeks after the fiscal year has commenced—there can be no reliable estimate of how total expenditures will compare with anticipated receipts. Several attempts have been made to correct the situation, but all have failed.

Early in the Eisenhower Administration, the Secretary of the Treasury and the Budget Director proposed a plan under which appropriations would be approved by the various appropriations committees on a tentative basis. Then, when all appropriations had received this tentative approval they would be brought together in an over-all budget. A special committee, composed of the chairmen of the appropriations and tax committees, would compare the totals with the latest estimates of receipts and make recommendations to the appropriations committees. These committees would then review the tentative budgets in light of the revenue situation before reaching a final decision.

Under this plan no power would be taken away from the appropriations committees, but Congress and the country would know before the budget was finally approved what the net result would be and the extent of the surplus or deficit. This proposal was rejected by the appropriations committees.

Another proposal, which has twice been approved by the Senate but has yet to clear the House, would establish a joint Congressional committee on the budget. Such a committee would consist of an equal number of Senators and Congressmen from the appropriations committees, and it would retain an adequate staff of experts to analyze the Departments' and agencies' requests and trends. The staff would also serve the appropriations committees and sub-committees. By holding joint hearings on budget requests, the proposed committee could obtain the views of interested groups and of those representing the general public. In cooperation with the Joint Committee on Internal Revenue, which now conducts extensive studies on tax policies, it could compare estimated expenditures and receipts. The success of the Joint Committee on Internal Revenue offers a clear precedent for such a joint committee on the budget.

Some plan along these lines would seem to be necessary to secure better control of the federal government's finances.

4

DECISION MAKING IN A
CABINET DEPARTMENT

As illustrations of the executive organization and decision-making functions of a Cabinet Department, I shall describe briefly the operations of the U. S. Treasury during the period 1953 to 1955, in which I served as Under Secretary, and the Department of Health, Education, and Welfare during the period of 1955 to 1958, when I served as Secretary. While the services performed by Cabinet Departments vary widely, these two illustrate the range of activities and the nature of the problems faced by a Secretary. At the time, each had over 50,000 employees.

THE UNITED STATES TREASURY

The Treasury includes a wide variety of agencies. Not only is it concerned with the collection of taxes, the disbursement of government funds, and the management of the public debt, but it also administers a number of bureaus. These include Engraving and Printing, the Mint, the Secret

Service, Customs, Narcotics, and the United States Coast Guard. A highly trained corps of civil servants has been developed over the years to administer these agencies.

Secretary Humphrey, so that he could devote as much time as possible to the general over-all fiscal and monetary policies of the Administration, organized the Department in a manner generally followed by chief executives of large business organizations. He divided the responsibility for administration between the Under Secretary, the Under Secretary for Monetary Affairs, an Assistant Secretary, and the General Counsel. The Secretary told each of us that we were responsible for the areas delegated to us and we should come to him only if there were policy questions with which he should be familiar or for his advice and decision where necessary.

We found it was not necessary to take up much of his time on day-to-day administrative problems. He did not hold regular staff conferences, but he and his principal assistants generally had lunch together to discuss current matters. The bureau heads were frequently brought in to participate in the discussion.

Thus the Secretary was freed from many of the administrative details and was able to devote a considerable part of his time to general policy questions relating to tax and monetary affairs, to confer with the President and other Cabinet members on Administration policies and programs, to keep in close touch with the key Senators and Congressmen, and to appear before Congressional committees. He also had time to meet with other groups and individuals on the outside, especially those concerned with tax policies and debt management. While he had few "press conferences" as such, he met frequently with members of the press, either singly or in groups.

The Department under his organization was able to function well and efficiently with a reduction of staff personnel. The principal assistants had several staff men working directly with them, but the Secretary had only one staff man. There was a central research and analysis staff which provided data on both tax and monetary matters for the Secretary and his principal assistants.

To illustrate how policies are formed and decisions reached, I shall trace an actual piece of legislation—the Income Tax Revision Act of 1954—from the inception of the idea to the signing of the bill by the President.

Case Study—Income Tax Law of 1954. For several years prior to 1953, many businessmen and others had been advocating reform in the tax laws, especially with a view to encouraging capital investment and removing some of the inequities. I was familiar with these views because of my service as chairman of the Tax Committee of the Business Advisory Council and as chairman of the Committee for Economic Development. I accepted the responsibility for developing a tax program in December 1952, at the time I agreed to become Under Secretary. One of my first steps was to obtain two able assistants—Professor Dan Throop Smith, of the Harvard Business School, to head up the tax analysis staff, and Kenneth Gemmill, of Philadelphia, to supervise the legal work.

In our first conference with the chairman of the Ways and Means Committee and his chief staff man, the Secretary and I learned that they were considering plans to recodify the whole income tax law as well as to carry out certain reforms. There had been no major revision of the code in seventy-five years; the law had been amended many times and there was great need to rearrange, consolidate, and clarify the various provisions. We readily agreed to combine forces and work with the Congressional group. Almost fifty working subcommittees were set up to deal with separate parts of the code, with representatives from the analysis and legal staffs of the Treasury, the Internal Revenue Service, and the Congressional staff. This highly technical process of recodification took several months of intensive work.

We were advised by some not to undertake the technical recodification at the same time we were recommending major changes. The Secretary decided, nevertheless, that we should take advantage of the opportunity when Congress and the Administration were so thoroughly in accord. This judgment has proved to be correct.

In the meantime, my two assistants and I discussed with many people the major revisions to be recommended. We conferred with members of the Council of Economic Advisers, the special assistant to the President for economic affairs, economists of other government agencies, and numerous other persons both in and out of government. The Secretary also met with many groups. We finally agreed upon about twenty principal revisions.

In reaching his decisions as to specific provisions to be recommended to the President and to Congress, the Secretary had to consider many factors. The corporation excess profits tax was to expire in January 1954—at the President's request this scheduled expiration had been postponed from July 1953—and the last increase in individual income taxes, enacted during the Korean War, was to be eliminated on January 1, 1954. These changes would result in the loss of about $5 billion in revenue. Thus we were severely limited in the extent to which our recommendations could cause additional loss of revenue. We had to confine our recommendations primarily to those proposals which would remove the most serious inequities in the individual income tax and concentrate on the features relating to corporation income tax which would have the greatest effect on removing obstacles to growth of the economy.

As far as business was concerned, the major measures proposed were:

1. faster depreciation during the early years of an asset;
2. steps toward reducing the double taxation of dividends;
3. treatment of research and development expenditures as either current expenses or capital items;
4. a more reasonable plan relating to the accumulation of surplus; and
5. a longer period for carry-back of losses.

We also had a number of recommendations to remove certain inequities in individual income taxes, such as the removal of the ceiling of $600 on a child's earnings for an exemption to the parent.

The Secretary and I, in the latter part of 1953, had a long conference with the President to explain the principal recommendations and reach agreement on most of the changes. I was particularly impressed with the quickness of President Eisenhower's mind in grasping the principal points in connection with our corporate income tax proposals, especially in view of the fact that he had had no previous experience with such matters.

We then presented the major tax proposals to the Cabinet members for their information and opinion. Our staff was working with the staff at the White House, the Council of Economic Advisers, and the Bureau of the Budget in the preparation of a message which the President would send to Congress to present the specific recommendations. Before the message went to Congress, the Secretary and I discussed the proposals at length with the legislative leaders.

The Ways and Means Committee had conducted extensive hearings in previous years and many people had given their views about the changes that should be made in the tax laws. The committee therefore did not consider it necessary to have further hearings on the President's recommendations. During 1954 the committee held executive sessions over an extended period of time to consider not only the principal items of reform which the President and others had recommended, but the detailed revision in the code upon which the fifty committees had been working. Our two principal assistants in the Treasury, along with the members of the Congressional Internal Revenue staff, participated in these deliberations.

After many months of work, the bill was finally reported out by the committee. During the process, the committee made a number of changes in the specific proposals we had presented and it was necessary for my staff and me to keep in close touch with the deliberations. We often called upon the Secretary to decide what views should be expressed to the committee. The bill was passed by the House after one or two close votes on certain provisions.

The Senate Committee on Finance conducted extensive hearings on the House bill, and the Secretary and I appeared before the committee to present our program. While the bill was being discussed in the House, we found that few Congressmen outside of those on the committee were familiar with the proposals, except for one or two major items. We therefore arranged for a series of meetings with the Republican Senators to explain to them the principal features. We also discussed these proposals with key Democratic Senators. As a result, when the bill came before the Senate for discussion, our proposals were fairly well understood. The Senate changed the House bill in several respects, but a compromise was worked out in conference. The bill was signed by the President in August 1954, one year and nine months after we started to work on it. On the whole, we were able to obtain about 75 percent of our principal recommendations, with which we were quite pleased.

One of the goals of the Congressmen and the Treasury was to simplify the code, but we found this exceedingly difficult because of the danger of opening up more loopholes. As an illustration, one rather serious mistake was made when we attempted to simplify the treatment of deferred income and expenses. Wrong estimates of the revenue loss were made not only by our staff but by several accountants in industry whom we had consulted. When we realized the situation, the Secretary acknowledged the mistake and got Congress to correct it immediately.

I might mention here that, at the time, there was opposition to one of the revisions—that which enabled business to make larger provisions for depreciation during the early

83

years of an asset. This opposition has died down now, and it is generally recognized that the changes in depreciation allowances have contributed to the generally high level of private investment since 1954. In fact, most people now feel that we should go further in accelerating depreciation. The most common complaint is that the length of useful life of equipment estimated by the Revenue Service is not realistic and does not adequately reflect the obsolescence factor. This is a matter which can be handled to a large extent by the Internal Revenue Service through a change in its regulations.

No major changes—and relatively few minor ones—have been made in the tax law since the act was passed. Yet there are still a number of major revisions that should be made.

A change in structure of the individual income tax system is probably the most needed reform. It is now generally agreed that a downward revision of these rates, especially in the higher and middle brackets, would be a stimulating factor for the growth of the economy.

Many experts also feel that we should not depend so much on the individual income taxes but should raise more revenue by broadly based excise taxes which would replace the existing selective excise taxes. The efforts of Secretary Humphrey to obtain interest in such a tax revision to raise only the same revenue as with the existing system were unavailing with the leaders of both Parties.

The Treasury, under the Eisenhower Administration, had several proposals in mind to recommend for major reforms, but the budget situation at no time after 1954 permitted a reduction in revenue. It was felt also that the surpluses which were achieved in the fiscal years 1956 and 1957 should be applied on the public debt.

THE DEPARTMENT OF HEALTH, EDUCATION, AND WELFARE

This Department covers a wide variety of activities under five major agencies—Public Health Service, Office of Education, Social Security Administration (including the Children's Bureau), Food and Drug Administration, and Office of Vocational Rehabilitation. Each of these agencies operates a number of programs, most of which are undergoing constant change. These programs affect many people, and the members of Congress are naturally quite interested in them.

A different type of organization from that of the Treasury is required. In the Treasury, the programs and procedures of the bureaus and agencies are well established, with rather infrequent legislative changes needed, except in the tax field. In the Department of Health, Education, and Welfare the Secretary must spend considerable time with legislation—with changes in existing programs, development of new programs, and the follow-through with Congress.

With this in mind, I arranged for the agency heads to report directly to me and I delegated as much authority and responsibility to them as possible. They would discuss policy questions and program matters with me, but only the more important administrative measures.

I used the Under Secretary as a line officer to supervise the administration of the Department and to assist me in all major matters. One Assistant Secretary was concerned with legislation and Congressional liaison; the other was a line officer to supervise the field organization of the various agencies. I had a Special Assistant for Health and Medical Affairs, one Assistant to the Secretary in my immediate office, another for Public Affairs, and a third for Program Analysis. With the exception of the Under Secretary and one Assistant Secretary, these assistants served primarily as staff officers for research, analysis, liaison, and follow-up with the agencies and Congress.

Important to the decision-making process of the Secretary is the collection and analysis of facts by the research staff of each of his Department's agencies. A small specialized staff under one of the assistants was concerned mainly with coordination of programs, special investigations, and follow-up of the agency activities.

I also kept in close touch with the director of administration (now Administrative Assistant Secretary)—a civil servant who was in charge of the day-to-day administration of the Department.

Incidentally, I should mention that I was very fortunate to obtain a group of able and dedicated assistants for both the line and staff appointive positions, and to have an equally able and dedicated group in the top Civil Service positions.

I held a weekly conference, attended by the agency heads and my principal assistants, to discuss programs and issues affecting the several agencies, to coordinate activities, and to exchange information. These conferences proved to be very helpful and accomplished much the same purpose as the meetings of a management advisory committee in business (see pages 19 and 20).

The agency heads would generally discuss specific problems and proposals with me directly rather than present them in the staff meetings. At these meetings they would discuss matters of general interest and also bring up problems of their own agencies on which they wanted to obtain advice.

As an illustration, we had several discussions of the problems of water pollution, on which some of the staff were working and which affected several agencies. The problem was what role the federal government should play in meeting the situation caused by water pollution. This is a question of growing importance—whether the role of the federal government should be limited to research to develop methods which the local communities can adopt or, in view of the fact that polluted streams affect many cities and often go through several states, whether the federal government should make small matching grants to the localities as an incentive for action.

These meetings provided me a good opportunity to keep my principal associates informed of current developments in the Cabinet, the White House, and Congress and also for them to keep me informed of the progress in their work. In discussing proposed programs here and in other groups, it was very helpful to have both the staff and the line people participate, and also the people in the line organization below the agency head. I found that I could obtain more information from the people who were most expert in a particular field and also that the wider participation in the decision-making process tended to raise morale generally.

In addition to these weekly meetings, I had almost daily luncheons with my immediate assistants and frequently invited the agency heads or others to join us.

I endeavored to operate the Department in the same informal manner that Secretary Humphrey used in the Treasury, but because of the diversity of programs and the need for constant contact with Congress, I could not delegate as much to my principal assistants as he did. I used these assistants more as staff men, with the agency heads reporting to me and the Under Secretary directly.

Budget Matters. The budget is the mechanism by which the Secretary develops programs and controls expenditures. It also provides an opportunity for him and his staff to determine what programs can be curtailed or possibly eliminated.

At the time I was Secretary, the Department's budget expenditures were about $3 billion, with a great number of individual items. (The Social Security trust fund expenditures, totaling about $10 billion annually, are outside the budget.)

The Secretary must become familiar with all important items in the budget, as he is called on to defend them before the Budget Bureau, the President, and Congressional committees. I appointed a budget committee, with the Under Secretary as chairman, to consider the budget requests before they were presented to me. If the agency heads and the budget committee could not agree, then the Under Secretary, the Director of Administration, the budget officer, and I would discuss the matter with the agency head to iron out differences.

In the meantime, the top Budget Bureau officials had received reports from their investigators assigned to the Department. Several conferences were generally necessary before the Budget Bureau director and I were able to reach agreement. If we could not agree, the major differences were taken to the White House for decision.

The budget matters required a considerable part of my time. I needed to give particularly careful thought to each item of the budget because decisions had to be made a year in advance; and once the "line item" budget is approved by Congress there is no opportunity to shift funds from one program to another, or even within the principal elements of a program. Efforts to obtain a small fund which could be used at the discretion of the Secretary have generally been unavailing.

If the Department of Health, Education, and Welfare is to perform the service required by the legislation establishing its programs, its expenditures will naturally have to increase as the economy and population expand. I soon found it very useful, in my conferences with the President and Congressional leaders, to supplement the dollar figures with a table showing the cost in relation to the gross national product. Upon hearing my requests for increases in some of the important programs—medical research, aid to medical schools, vocational rehabilitation, and the Food and Drug Administration—some former associates in the Treasury and the Budget Bureau wondered if I had not changed my views about fiscal soundness. I recall that Secretary Humphrey made a remark in a Cabinet meeting that it didn't take long for the Treasury influence to wear off. I assured him, however, that I had not changed my views at all, but was only facing up to the most pressing needs.

I was quite impressed with the careful scrutiny given to the details of the budget by the Congressional appropriations subcommittees. In most cases they reduced the amounts asked for.

A striking exception occurred, however, in the case of medical research. Over the past few years the committees have appropriated considerably larger sums than requested by the President. The limiting factor in the growth of medical research has been the shortage of trained scientists to do the research work. Fortunately, the people who initiated the Institutes of Health program a few years ago had the foresight to provide funds for training research workers, and many more research workers are now available. We are still spending a relatively small amount of the total research dollar for medical research, and expenditures in this particularly important field should increase as more research workers become available.

Case Study—National Defense Education Act of 1958. As a case study to illustrate the workings of this Department, I have chosen the enactment of the National Defense Education Act of 1958, which authorized the expenditure of approximately $1 billion to assist schools, colleges, and students in a number of different ways, over a period of four years.

The White House Conference on Education, held in the fall of 1955, made recommendations for improving our public schools in many respects. One of the principal recommendations—a program for federal aid for classroom construction—was endorsed by President Eisenhower, but Congress defeated bills proposed by the Administration in 1956 and again in 1957. This legislation was approved by the Senate but had run into difficulty in the House. The 1957 bill was defeated even though both Party platforms in the Presidential campaign of 1956 expressly approved federal aid for classroom construction.

In a discussion with the President after Congress had adjourned in 1957, we agreed that the classroom proposal probably would again be defeated by the same Congress in 1958, and we should therefore prepare another type of program concentrating on improvement in science and mathematics. We still were convinced of the need for classroom aid and hoped to have such a bill passed later.

Immediately after my conference with the President, I set up a task force, composed of staff men from the Office of Education and some of my own assistants, to develop a broad program for improvement in not only these two areas but in other critical areas in which there was a clear national interest.

Early in 1956, at my suggestion, the President had appointed a Committee on Education Beyond the High School, which the following year submitted its recommendations for strengthening higher education.

In reaching a decision as to which of the many proposals endorsed by the educators I should recommend to the President, several factors had to be considered. First and foremost, in view of the record of the House in refusing for years to go along with a general federal aid program, we had to be careful to avoid getting into the issues which had caused this opposition. We had to demonstrate that there was a clear national interest in each proposal and that action by the federal government was necessary. We also had to work with a limited budget because of the tight budget situation for the government as a whole. I had to keep in mind what I thought I could persuade the President

91

was necessary and, also, what I thought Congress would be likely to approve. I had to guard against the natural enthusiasm of educators, both in and outside the government. I had to avoid programs that would run counter to the President's strong views that the federal government should not interfere with the functions of state and local governments. In addition, I had to keep in mind the general fear of "federal control of education." Each proposal was considered in the light of these criteria.

There naturally were differences of opinion among the individuals in the Department. For instance, I remember that there was a sharp difference of opinion as to whether, in our proposals to overcome the shortages in the fields of science and mathematics, we should make grants to stimulate premium pay for teachers in these fields. This was turned down because we felt that it would be an undesirable educational practice, and furthermore it was not politically feasible.

After we had narrowed the field down to six or eight tentative proposals, we called in a number of consultants in the educational field, including several college and university presidents and public school superintendents, to give us their opinion of the program as a whole and, particularly, of the program in which they were best informed. We had two purposes in view: one was to double check the judgment of our own Office of Education staffs, and the other was to win advance support for our proposals. I sat in on many of these discussions to be sure that I would understand the various viewpoints. We made a number of changes as the result of the advice of these outside consultants. Such a procedure is generally very helpful, as it is seldom advisable for a Secretary to rely solely on his agency staff, no matter how competent.

We also discussed the proposals at length with the White House staff, particularly the newly appointed special assistant to the President for science. The appearance of the first sputnik in October 1957 gave great impetus to the movement to strengthen the teaching of science and math and to bolster education generally.

The program which we then submitted to the President included the following principal proposals:

1. grants to the states for improvement in the teaching of math, science, and modern foreign languages;

2. grants to the states for improvement in testing, guidance, and counseling in the high schools to prevent the loss of able students who fail to complete their studies;

3. grants to colleges and universities for the establishment of institutes for training teachers in modern foreign languages, especially the rare languages;

4. fellowships to graduate students and accompanying grants to the graduate schools, designed primarily to increase the number of college teachers;

5. a program of scholarships for able high-school graduates to be selected by individual states on the basis of merit and need.

The proposals were then presented to President Eisenhower with charts and facts to justify each one. He generally agreed with the proposals, even though they were greatly expanded from those he and I had discussed originally. But he was concerned about the total cost of the program in view of the tight budget situation. Later, in working with the Budget Bureau, we reduced certain features to bring down the cost.

At the President's suggestion, I presented the whole program to the Cabinet for the members' information and suggestions, and there was general agreement for the program. We then proceeded, under the leadership of the Assistant Secretary, to prepare a draft of the proposed legislation.

In December I went to Gettysburg to discuss the final plan with the President, including the cost estimates and an outline for his message to Congress. After obtaining his approval, the press secretary and I held a press conference in which we gave a summary of the program.

This press conference was well attended by the White House correspondents and, as this was the only news item reported from the White House that day, our story got front-page coverage in all the principal daily papers. We later collected clippings, especially editorials, from papers throughout the country and found a very high percentage in favor of our proposals. This was very helpful to me later on in developing Congressional support for the program.

Our staff worked with the White House staff in preparing the message for the President to present to Congress in January. We also discussed the program with the legislative leaders. The bill covering our proposals was introduced in both houses immediately after the message was presented.

As both houses of Congress were controlled by the Democrats, it was necessary for me to work closely with the leaders of that Party to obtain their cooperation in getting the legislation through. Thus the situation was unlike that of 1954 when we were dealing with our own Party in obtaining the tax legislation. I anticipated little difficulty in the Senate as to general approval of the program, but I knew there would be much discussion of the details.

Soon after I became Secretary I had developed close and cordial relations with the chairman of the Senate Committee on Labor and Public Welfare, Senator Lister Hill of Alabama, and the ranking Republican member, Senator H. Alexander Smith of New Jersey—both able Senators of long, dedicated service. Senator Hill was also chairman of the appropriations subcommittee which dealt with our budget.

I had joint conferences with Senators Hill and Smith in the fall of 1957 and kept them in close touch with the program as it developed. I found that they were generally sympathetic to the proposals. Senator Hill later introduced a bill of his own, following in general the outlines of our bill but increasing the amounts authorized and incorporating some new features.

The situation in the House was difficult, as the chairman of the committee was generally opposed to federal aid to education. Fortunately, the chairman of the subcommittee on education, Congressman Carl Elliott of Alabama, was very much in sympathy with the whole program. Soon after our bill was introduced, he introduced another bill following the general lines of ours, but with several proposals expanded and new features added. Our staff immediately began working with the Congressman and the staff of his subcommittee to agree upon compromise proposals. I personally worked closely with the members of the subcommittee during this process.

During the discussion it developed that there was considerable sentiment among the Republican members of the committee for a student loan program in addition to scholarships. The Assistant Secretary had conferences with officials of several large universities administering loan programs and devised a plan which met with the approval of these members. In a conference with these Republican Congressmen and our staff, the President agreed to support both the loan program and the scholarship program.

In appearing before the Senate and House committees to explain the proposals, I was particularly careful to point out that the program was not intended in any way to supplant the local and private effort, but to serve as a stimulus for action in a few specific but very important areas where greater effort was necessary in the national interest.

For instance, to support our proposals for early counseling and scholarships, I pointed out that each year over 200,000 young people, with high ranking in their classes, are lost to advanced education, resulting in the waste of part of our most vital resources.

To support our recommendation for aid to the states to assist local districts in supplying equipment for the teaching of science and mathematics, I pointed out that only one out of three of our high-school graduates had taken chemistry; one out of four, physics; and only one out of eight, trigonometry or solid geometry. I also mentioned that while every state had supervisors at the state level to assist the local districts in approving their courses in vocational education (because of the aid received through the Vocational Education Act of 1917), only three states had such supervisors in the field of mathematics and only seven in the field of science. We proposed that funds be granted to the states to provide such supervisory personnel to help the local systems improve their curriculum and methods.

In support of our proposal for grants to graduate teachers, I gave the estimate of the needs for college teachers for the next ten years and indicated how inadequate the supply of Ph.D.'s was. To support our recommendation for improvement in the teaching of foreign languages, I stated that we were probably the most backward major nation in the world in the vital field of language competence and that only about 15 percent of our high-school students were studying foreign languages.

After extensive hearings the House committee reported out a bill covering most of the President's recommendations, including both the scholarship and loan proposals and additional programs for new area vocational schools and for research into new educational media.

The chief subject of debate on the floor of the House was whether there should be a scholarship program or a loan program. The scholarship program was criticized on the basis that everyone should pay for his own education and that a loan fund was sufficient. It was not clearly brought out in the debate that an important objective of scholarships based on merit and need was to create a greater incentive for academic achievement. Although the scholarship program had been endorsed by a substantial majority of the committee members, the floor vote was adverse after only short debate. This was a last-minute floor change, illustrating the danger that all legislation runs. However, it was the only major change in the committee's recommendations and the bill was passed by the House.

The Senate committee also held a series of hearings. I met with the committee members quite frequently after the hearings were concluded in an attempt to work out a compromise between Senator Hill's bill and the Administration bill. We were generally agreed in principle but not as to the amounts of authorization. A satisfactory bill was reported out, but with a modified scholarship program with the hope of winning over the House conferees.

I was also asked to testify before the Foreign Affairs Committee, which was particularly interested in the provisions to stimulate the teaching of foreign languages. In spite of all the homework which a Secretary does in preparing for an appearance before a committee, he is often caught flatfooted by a question. For instance, in appearing before this committee the first question asked me by 90-year-old Senator Green, then chairman of the committee and still quite keen, was "Mr. Secretary, what is the purpose of education?" With so many experts and educators from the Department in the room, I had to be very careful in my reply. I responded to the effect that in my opinion the purpose of education was to enable an individual to develop to his greatest potential capacity and thereby help himself and his country. I was relieved to find later that the experts in the Department did not seem to be dissatisfied with the answer.

The Senate and House conferees finally agreed with the House proposals and eliminated the scholarship plan. With this exception, a high percentage of the original recommendations were accepted by Congress, with some additional features incorporated.

An amendment was added to the bill on the floor of the

Senate, just before passage, requiring a loyalty oath and a non-communist affidavit from all applicants for loans under the student loan provision. Objection was raised to this amendment, but it was being considered in the closing days of the session and in the rush to adjourn it was agreed to by the Senate and the conferees. This amendment, especially the affidavit, has caused considerable criticism among educators, and a few institutions have declined to go along with the program. In fact, both the Eisenhower and Kennedy Administrations have recommended the repeal of the affidavit provision. This incident illustrates the risk of passing a floor amendment which is not thoroughly considered by the respective committees.

The bill as a whole, however, was the most comprehensive federal-aid-to-education bill since the land-grant college act was passed in 1862. Thanks to the efforts of many members of both Parties in Congress, we were able to avoid some of the issues which had defeated attempts at federal aid in the past.

Educators are generally agreed that the results of the program have been satisfactory and that it should be continued.* Some recommend that the program be expanded to include assistance in the teaching of English as well as mathematics, science, and foreign languages, and also that the fellowship program for graduate studies be expanded.

* The present Congress has extended the act for two years beyond June 30, 1962.

HOW EFFICIENTLY ARE FEDERAL DEPARTMENTS RUN?

Good progress has been made in certain federal Departments in adopting more modern and up-to-date office methods. Sometimes this progress has been accomplished by surveys conducted by task forces set up within a Department. In other cases outside consultants and technicians familiar with the best procedures in business and industry have been helpful. Competent specialists in a particular field can usually be obtained for a short period of time without difficulty. In any event, there is generally room for improvement in large government Departments, just as there is in large business organizations.

While I was Under Secretary of the Treasury we were able to obtain a thorough engineering survey of the Bureau of Engraving and Printing by an outside engineering concern and to obtain the part-time services of three outstanding men in the printing industry to assist us in evaluating the results of the survey and in reaching decisions on the recommendations made. The results were very satisfying.

In order to obtain an objective appraisal of the operation of the Social Security Administration, I appointed in 1957 a group of consultants with wide experience in large-scale operations in industry and insurance. The following are excerpts from their report:

The consultants believe that the bureau is carrying out its mission in a sound and vigorous manner. . . . The bureau has been a pioneer in the very difficult matter of introducing automatic machinery into the paperwork area with substantial savings to the trust funds.

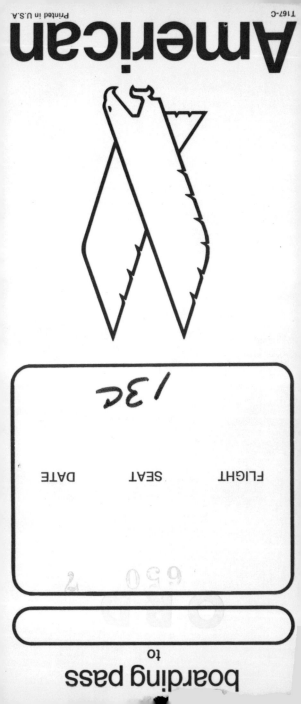

The consultants were impressed with the quality of the staff, which compares quite favorably with the staffs of corresponding business organizations.

The consultants made several suggestions for improvement which were adopted. It is interesting to note that the over-all expenses of this operation are now less than 2 percent of the benefits paid, a ratio which stands up well compared with the experience of large insurance operations.

The Budget Bureau, which is responsible for studying management procedures and making recommendations to the Departments, could do a more thorough job than at present if it had a more adequate staff to make these studies. The bureau also could well do more long-range planning on its own and encourage such planning on the part of the agencies and Departments. Long-range forecasts are needed particularly for many programs which are modest at the beginning but which have the potential of developing into much heavier expenditures in the years ahead.

5

DECISION MAKING IN A CONGRESSIONAL COMMITTEE

No treatise about the process of decision making in government would be complete without a discussion of the role of Congress. Congress, of course, occupies the key decision-making role in our federal government. While the legislative process seems at times unwieldy and long, it is, on the whole, thorough and democratic. And, as demonstrated through the years, speed can be obtained when vitally necessary.

Rather than discuss in general terms the way in which Congress formulates policies and arrives at decisions, I thought it would be more interesting and informative to describe the successful functioning of a Congressional committee in handling an important and complex problem. I have chosen the War Contract Termination Act of 1944.

CASE STUDY—WAR CONTRACT
TERMINATION ACT OF 1944

In the spring of 1944, the House of Representatives established a Special Committee on Postwar Economic Policy and Planning, under the chairmanship of Congressman William M. Colmer. This group was directed to make recommendations to the regular committees of Congress for legislation needed to facilitate the orderly demobilization and reconversion after the war. I was staff director of this committee during its life of three years.

I have previously remarked on the use of executive staff in analyzing and investigating a problem, in collecting facts, in presenting the major factors involved to the executive concerned, in developing the various possible courses of action, and in assisting with the appraisal of these alternatives. A Congressional committee staff does this work.

Soon after this special committee was organized, the chairman and I, finding that there was a confused situation concerning legislation in regard to the termination of war contracts, felt that the special committee should give immediate study to this problem. I was familiar with the general nature of the problem as a result of the work of the Committee for Economic Development. At that time, industry and the military Departments were very interested in seeing that an effective plan be set up for the prompt termination of war contracts so that plants could be readily converted back to peacetime production and employment. After the First World War many months and years had gone by before contracts were finally settled. Much unemployment resulted.

In 1944, business organizations and the military Departments had generally agreed upon a specific program, and a bill incorporating these recommendations had been introduced in the Senate.

In the House there was strong sentiment for having the Comptroller General audit all settlements before they became final. The Military Affairs Committee had reported out a bill giving this authority to the Comptroller General. The Naval Affairs Committee had reported out a bill giving the Comptroller General limited authority. It was the opinion of industry and of the contracting officers of the military Departments that either one of these bills would cause considerable delays in reconversion and re-employment.

The task of our committee was to develop a satisfactory program and obtain the approval of a majority of the members of the House. We were handicapped, as are all special committees, by the lack of jurisdiction to report legislation. We would have to depend upon the standing committees for action on any bill we might develop. Our committee, however, was composed of eighteen ranking members from important committees of the House, and a report from such a representative committee should have considerable influence. As staff director, I began to furnish information on the subject to the members of the committee, but I had difficulty getting them to read the reports because of other pressures on their time. I then learned the value of Congressional hearings.

We planned a series of hearings at which important men from industry and the accounting profession, along with representatives of the military Departments, explained the difficult problems involved and the need for prompt settlements. Attendance of the Congressmen at the hearings was very good, particularly when key executives were testifying, and before the hearings were concluded the members became well acquainted with the problem.

At the suggestion of the automobile companies, several members visited Detroit and went through one of the plants which had been making tanks but which had been completely closed down because a better model had been developed. This gave a practical demonstration of the complexities of the problem of settling a contract and clearing out a plant. I found out that two Congressmen on the committee had never been inside a large industrial plant before. This helps to illustrate the need for businessmen to take a greater personal interest in their local Congressmen—for the benefit of the whole community.

Following the hearings a subcommittee, consisting of members with legal experience, was appointed to draft a bill. This subcommittee held more than twenty executive sessons over a period of three weeks, each session running two or three hours. Assistant Secretaries from the War and the Navy Departments—men who were concerned with contracts—attended the meetings to explain details and answer questions.

The subcommittee finally completed its draft, which included a number of changes from the Senate bill. The provision relating to the detection of fraud was strengthened, but otherwise the Comptroller General was not given authority to pre-audit the agreements.

The committee chairman and I had a conference with the Comptroller General to obtain more specific information regarding his fears that there might be widespread fraud in case our bill was enacted. The Comptroller General had authority all during the war to audit cost-plus contracts and yet he cited to us only a few minor instances of fraud. As a result of this favorable experience we concluded that there would be little likelihood of widespread fraud. Neither did he convince the committee, when he appeared before it, that pre-audit was necessary.

The full committee gave its approval to the subcommittee's draft with only a few changes and the staff was asked to prepare a report explaining the bill. By this time, the members were all convinced of the need for quick action in settling contracts if large-scale unemployment was to be avoided at the end of the war.

When the report was being discussed I was asked by one of the minority members (there were ten Democrats and eight Republicans) if I would assist in the preparation of the minority report. I expressed surprise that there would be two reports because there seemed to be little if any difference of opinion in the committee. I stated that if the committee could not get out a report on which there was general agreement on this nonpolitical problem which was so important to the country, it would not have much influence on legislation. I told him that I hoped we could get a unanimous report, but that each member would have the right to add a footnote of dissent to any particular recommendation. The Congressman agreed and a report was adopted unanimously. The question of a minority report was never again raised in this committee, although in the standing committees it is the general rule to have majority and minority reports.

The bill was introduced and referred to the Judiciary Committee, which reported it to the House with a few minor changes. The bill also received the approval of the chairman of the Naval Affairs Committee. Opposition developed on the floor of the House in support of the Comptroller General's position. But with the active support of our eighteen-man committee, the Judiciary Committee, and the chairman of the Naval Affairs Committee, the bill was passed by a substantial majority. There was little difficulty experienced in getting the Senate to go along with the House bill.

The speed with which contracts were settled and payments made to the contracting firms was one of the principal reasons why reconversion took place with much less confusion and unemployment than had been widely anticipated. One year after V-J Day this committee reported that 90 percent of contract settlements and 95 percent of plant clearances had been completed. This was in sharp contrast to the long drawn-out, much-criticized process following World War I ... and, of course, the volume of contracts after World War II was considerably greater.

The fears of the Comptroller General that there would be substantial fraud in turning over this responsibility to contracting officers were not borne out. There were very few instances of fraud.

During the 78th and 79th Congresses, this Postwar Planning Committee issued eleven reports, dealing with such subjects as the "Removal of Wartime Controls," "General Economic Problems of the Reconversion Period," "Postwar Foreign Economic Policy," and "Postwar Public

Works and Construction." A report on "Economic Recovery in Europe" was based upon a visit of seven members to Europe immediately following the war, during which they interviewed the top officials of the various countries. The report contained the first recommendations from a Congressional committee that this country assist in the recovery of Europe through loans and grants, and thus it actually blueprinted the pattern which subsequently developed.

The committee's work turned out to be very fruitful in the nation's process of planning for reconversion in the postwar period.

The principal conclusions to be drawn from this case study are that Congressional hearings constitute a very important part of the legislative process in informing members on all phases of the subject . . . that such a committee can do a thorough job . . . and that many members of Congress are competent, with a high sense of devotion to duty.

I recall that in a debate on the 1954 tax bill one of the Republican leaders, Congressman Charles A. Halleck, was to make a closing speech for the bill. He was not on the committee which drafted the bill and he knew about it only in a general way.

He asked our tax expert in the Treasury to spend about thirty minutes with him to discuss the principal features. As it turned out, the time permitted only ten minutes to go over a number of these complicated items. Yet the Congressman in his speech presented a good and accurate statement. I was so impressed with this feat that I looked up his record and found that he had graduated near the top of his class, with Phi Beta Kappa honors, from his state University of Indiana.

As a result of my experience as staff director of this special Congressional committee at the close of World War II and my subsequent contacts with Congress from the Executive Department, I came to have much more confidence in our legislative process. With the staff work, the hearings, the full discussions by subcommittees and committees in one House, and then with the same procedure by an entirely different group of people in the other House, the process is a thorough one, with plenty of opportunity for various viewpoints to be considered. Of course, the final result is generally a compromise . . . but is not this the democratic process?

STAFF NEEDS OF A
CONGRESSIONAL COMMITTEE

It is obvious that the collection and analysis of facts is just as important for a Congressional committee as for an executive in business or a federal Department Secretary. A competent staff is essential in this process.

While the Military and Tax Committees have adequate staffs, many other committees do not. Additional staffs for the important committees of both the House and the Senate would better ensure the committee members' having access to pertinent information. For example, with annual appropriations now in excess of $80 billion, it is especially important that the Appropriations Committee and its subcommittees be more adequately staffed.

The hearings on proposed legislation play an important role in this process. Hearings have been found, as in the case study, to be the most effective way of giving the committee members the viewpoints of the various groups who are affected by the proposed legislation as well as giving the public generally an opportunity to be heard.

As a rule, business leaders do not participate in these hearings to the extent that they should. They depend too much upon trade associations and lawyers or public relations men. A personal appearance of an important executive is far more effective, as much greater importance is attributed to what he has to say. The members of the committee are just as interested in the viewpoints of leading businessmen as other leaders. Businessmen are sometimes concerned about the kind of treatment they might receive, probably due to headlines given to isolated instances. But a businessman who knows his subject and presents a frank statement will be treated in a courteous manner.

The value of businessmen testifying before Congressional committees was dramatically brought home to me in 1935 when I made my first appearance before the Senate Committee on Finance while it was considering the original Social Security legislation. I had been one of the five employer members of the President's Advisory Council which had assisted in the development of these proposals.

I was asked by the other employer representatives to present our views before the committee and specifically to suggest some amendments in the bill which had passed the House but which differed in a number of respects from the recommendations of our Advisory Council.

I had assumed that the members of the committee understood the various provisions of the bill. It soon became apparent, however, that they did not and I had to spend considerable time explaining the particular provisions before I could refer to the amendments which we had in mind. The committee members were very interested and I spent practically the whole morning with them.

Shortly afterward, the chairman of the committee (Senator Pat Harrison) called me to his office and stated that this was a very complicated matter—as in fact it was. The bill covered not only unemployment insurance, old age insurance, and old age assistance, but several other titles setting up various grants-in-aid programs in the welfare field. The committee members had not had an opportunity, he told me, to study the bill carefully in view of the pressure of many other bills (this was in the early days of the New Deal). They had had two or three weeks of hearings but, he stated, either he and the other members were dumb or the experts couldn't express themselves, but they just could not understand what some of the previous witnesses were talking about. He said that I could speak the language they understood, and was the first witness to appear who had had practical experience in pension and unemployment benefits. He then asked me if I could indicate specifically the amendments which I would suggest. I had prepared the wording for different amendments and I went over each one of them, which he copied in his personal copy of the bill. Many of these changes were ultimately adopted.

This and subsequent advisory councils had much to do with developing the Social Security System and the sound and comprehensive programs which it now encompasses. The council appointed in 1937 by the the Social Security Board and the United States Senate Committee on Finance, the council appointed by the Senate Committee in 1947, and also the committee which was set up by the Eisenhower Administration in 1954 all presented recommendations which were, in most cases, approved unanimously by the members and which, to a large extent, were adopted by Congress in subsequent legislation.

Such councils, composed of representatives of employers, labor, and the general public, can perform a useful function in matters which require careful study by experts and balanced judgment by a representative group of interested citizens. It was my good fortune to serve on all these advisory councils on Social Security and I thus know at first hand the contributions they made to the development of the present system. It was a stimulating experience to serve on these councils. The members represented various viewpoints and yet when all the facts were on the table they were able to reach general agreement on most of the principal points at issue. Such councils supplement effectively the staff work of the Executive Departments and the staff work and hearings of the Congressional committees.

6

PROBLEMS IN BUILDING A
GOVERNMENT STAFF

In the final analysis, of course, the wisdom of all decisions and policies depends on the caliber and experience of the executive and his staff people. For this reason, I should like to explore some of the specialized problems government organizations face in recruiting executive personnel and in building effective staffs.

PROBLEMS IN THE FEDERAL GOVERNMENT

A particularly fundamental problem is pointed up by a simple comparison:

In business the chief executive's principal assistants are generally men who have devoted much of their business careers to that company, and if a vacancy occurs the executive usually has a choice between several able men.

In the federal government, however, when an Administration changes in four years—or now at the most, eight years—not only is the Secretary new but he has the responsibility of selecting his immediate assistants. In most cases, these people also are newcomers, often without any government experience. This presents the most serious problem of management in government.

On the other hand, the situation affords a splendid opportunity to bring new blood and fresh viewpoints to these key positions, to take a fresh look at existing programs and the proper organizations for carrying them out, to eliminate programs no longer necessary, and to initiate different approaches.

An influential Congressman of long service once told me that "The success or failure of an Administration is often determined by the caliber of the men whom the President brings in at the beginning of his Administration." He pointed out that history illustrates that this has been true of all heads of government, from biblical times down to the present. The history of our own country records a long list of brilliant Secretaries and advisers whom a new President had brought into public service and the competent assistants whom these men had in turn attracted.

In the administration of a Cabinet Department, the Secretary will rely upon two groups of management personnel: first, a small number of Presidential appointees and, second, those in the upper grades of Civil Service. The efficiency and effectiveness of government operations depend to a large extent upon these comparatively few men.

Progress has been made in recent years in reducing the turnover in top government personnel by increasing the positions which are brought under Civil Service and reducing the number of Presidential appointees. However, we have about reached the limit in the number who can be taken out of appointive positions and placed under Civil Service.

In a typical Department, the Presidential appointees are now generally limited to the Under Secretary, Assistant Secretaries, a few assistants and confidential secretaries, and a few bureau chiefs. Most of the appointive bureau chiefs and some of the Assistant Secretaries and others concerned with purely technical administrative matters could be placed under Civil Service, but the number would be limited. Most students of government agree that an Administration needs to select the top executives to ensure complete sympathy to its programs.

Attention is often called to the fact that in a change of government in England, no turnover takes place in the personnel of a Department with the exception of the Secretary and, in some cases, the Under Secretary. But the suggestion that we adopt such a plan fails to take into account the differences between the nature of our government and the parliamentary system of England.

Presidential Appointees. The recruitment of competent people for these key appointive positions is an important problem for a United States Secretary.

For suggestions the Secretary has to depend to a large extent upon his own acquaintances and friends, the White House, or upon the political leaders. He finds difficulty in obtaining the right person fitted by experience and qualifications for the particular job.

I was fortunate in being able to obtain, in most cases, exceptionally competent people for the key positions under my supervision, both in the Treasury and in the Department of Health, Education, and Welfare. I would generally obtain lists of prospects from acquaintances and others who knew people in the particular fields. I narrowed down these lists to a few persons whom I would check closely with outside sources and personally interview. This was generally a long drawn-out process, but it proved worthwhile and successful.

Although my experience as Secretary of the Department of Health, Education, and Welfare may have been unique, it was very seldom that I had any pressure from political organizations in filling these positions.

I recall one position which I had to fill because of the retirement of a person who had held that position for many years. Many organizations were interested in this bureau and we received a number of suggestions as to the type of person required and as to individuals. We compiled a long list of prospects and interviewed a number of them. After we had finally agreed upon a person, one of the press people wrote an article about the thorough process we had pursued in arriving at this selection. A day or two later I received a letter from Supreme Court Justice Felix Frankfurter, who had read this article and who said:

> The longer I observe affairs, the stronger I am of the view that the right question to ask about a public act is not "Is it right?" but rather "How was it reached?" Right or wrong largely rests in judgment. There are no available measurements by which one can obtain the right answer. Confidence in the wisdom of the judgment therefore must derive from confidence in the deliberative process and the disinterested inquiry that gave the result.

I should like you to know what confidence is aroused in me by your selection of the new Chief. I know nothing about _____ except what I have read since the appointment. What makes me confident that you have chosen wisely is the manner in which you went about it.

It is unfortunate that so much of a Secretary's time has to be devoted to recruiting his top personnel and that the length of stay is so short when he does succeed in locating an able man. The average length of service in appointive positions is probably less than two years. Quite often the executive leaves just about the time he is reaching his peak of usefulness.

Individuals for the top executive positions are generally recruited from one of four categories: businessmen, lawyers, college professors, and state and local government officials.

For certain executive positions a businessman with experience in handling people in large organizations is particularly well fitted. The older businessmen, recently retired or approaching retirement age, are sometimes available, but it is hard to obtain younger men in their late thirties or forties who have had ten or fifteen years of experience in important administrative positions in large business organizations.

In many cases, difficulty is experienced because of the difference in salaries and the possible loss of pension rights and other employee benefits. But difficulty is due even more to the young executive's fear that he would find upon his return from government service that he might have lost an opportunity for advancement.

On the other hand, it is probably true that government

117

experience would greatly benefit the individual and, indirectly, his company.

We had difficulty, both in the Treasury and in the Department of Health, Education, and Welfare, in recruiting such men from business. I recall one case in the Treasury where I had obtained the approval of the president and the chairman of a company for the release of a man for only six months for a special but very important assignment. He would have to be on the government payroll, however, and thus, for the time being, off the company payroll. The individual was willing but the directors of the company turned down the request because of complications in pension and stock option rights and because of the fear of setting a precedent. In a case in the Department of Health, Education, and Welfare I obtained approval of the president of a large company for release of an executive for two years. The president told the individual that he thought it would be good for both him and the company for him to accept. The man's immediate superior, however, was not so favorably inclined and I finally lost this prospect.

Employers could help the situation if they would maintain the status of the individual while he is in government service with regard to pension rights and other employee benefit plans. The government should make it clear in the regulations that such arrangements regarding benefit plans are permissible for men on leave of absence from their companies. The company could also help by assuring the individual that, although it can not promise to hold a particular position open, some appropriate position will be available to him when he returns, and every effort will be made to place him in a position at least as good as the one he previously had.

Sometimes company matters have nothing to do with refusals. I remember a situation where the company and the man were agreeable to his coming, but the man's wife objected because she didn't want to change schools for the children. Another time I located a man who had retired early although in good health. He was ideally fitted for the top position I had in mind and had previously served in Washington. But he finally decided he just didn't want to undertake the strenuous work and long hours generally required in these jobs.

As a rule, the businessman most likely to succeed in government work is one who has not only had his ability demonstrated by his previous progress, but one who has shown an interest in government policies and public affairs. He should have been active in affairs in his local community or in local and national trade organizations and thus have become familiar with the types of problems faced by government. It would also be very helpful if he had some previous experience with the federal government, either in part-time work or in service on advisory committees.

Securing good men from other fields is not so difficult as from the business field.

Lawyers with corporate law experience are well fitted by training and experience for many of these appointive positions—not just as general counsels in the Departments, but also as Assistant and Under Secretaries. This is especially true for the positions which call for contacts with members of Congress and the preparation and analysis of bills. Lawyers also are very helpful in analyzing problems and planning programs. Due to the nature of their experience, they are accustomed to adapting themselves to new situations. While not many lawyers are experienced in administrative or executive positions, this kind of ability is not always necessary. On the other hand, some young lawyers have turned out to be very able executives in government.

For many of these positions college professors, especially those in the fields of political science, economics, and business administration, are good prospects. Most of them have had little executive experience and desire staff rather than administrative positions. They can be valuable additions for most Departments and are especially helpful in formulating programs.

Good men are available also in other professions, such as hospital, health, and welfare administration. Experienced men sometimes can be drawn also from state and local governments. These government officials, however, probably would prefer Civil Service positions so they would not be subject to loss of status when Administrations change.

With so many able people available, the problem resolves itself into one of recruitment and proper placement. It would seem desirable to have the staff assistant in the White House who is concerned with personnel assist the Secretaries and agency heads in a systematic manner. He could maintain a list of various positions to be filled by Presidential appointees, with the job analysis and qualifications required for each position.

Over the years a file of qualified men could be compiled and it should be made known on the outside that key men interested in government service should contact this person. He would serve only in a staff or advisory capacity, as the actual selection would, of course, continue to be made by the President and the respective Secretary.

The personnel staff officer could also arrange for orientation programs for the new executives which would cover such things as conflict of interest, the mechanism of Civil Service, the differences between government and business operations, and the recommended approaches in dealing with Congress.

The federal government could also help matters by clarifying the conflict-of-interest issue. In most cases there is no conflict of interest, but a few outstanding cases have caused undue concern. The difficulty generally occurs only in the few Departments, such as Defense, which are concerned with procurement.

This question of conflict of interest is now in a great state of confusion and complexity due to the number of statutes relating to various phases of the problem, some of which go back many years. The situation would be alleviated to a great extent if these statutes could be consolidated and a reasonable statute adopted to meet present conditions. A comprehensive program to this end has been developed by a committee of the New York Bar Association, and President Kennedy has recently submitted to Congress some proposals to help the situation. It should also be made clear that the usual rules regarding outside connections and income do not apply in the case of part-time, temporary consultants, who can be of much value to the Departments.

In considering the qualities needed for a person to succeed in the appointive positions, I should point out that it is not enough for an individual to be competent; he must also have the ability to explain his position and convince others. An individual will find that government service in these positions will generally be satisfying, and that the insight gained into the workings of the federal government will broaden his outlook and be otherwise helpful in his future career.

While the salaries of the appointive positions are satisfactory to some of the persons concerned, they are a handicap in attracting many others. Although the government cannot, for a number of reasons, compete with industry, it is felt that a reasonable increase in the salaries of the top positions would remove some of the present handicaps. The cost would be slight because only about 300 positions at the Under Secretary and Assistant Secretary levels would be affected.

Civil Service. It is particularly desirable that maximum salaries in the top grades of Civil Service also be raised. These maximum salaries are distinctly out of line with comparable positions in industry, although the salaries of government employees in the lower and medium grades compare favorably with those for similar work in industry. The employee benefits now also compare well with progressive companies in industry.

The salary situation is particularly acute in the three top grades, which cover about 1,500 people. Salaries are also out of line in many of the scientific and technical positions which are becoming increasingly important. The government is losing too many of the people in these grades. Employees generally reach these positions when their children are of college age, and the higher salaries available elsewhere are often too attractive to decline. An increase in salary would not only enable more of them to stay in government service but could attract a larger number of well-qualified young people to government service in the first place.

During the 1930's, government careers and salaries were attractive enough for the government to obtain its full share of able college graduates. This has not been the case in the postwar years, however, because of competition from industry and the professions.

While the salary situation has been a handicap, it is encouraging to know that a high percentage of the top Civil Service people continue on and render dedicated service even though they know they have reached the government's maximum salary limit and could command a higher salary in industry.

There are certain attractions in these positions—security for one thing, but even more, the knowledge that the position offers the opportunity to perform a constructive service for the country. And the work itself can be stimulating and broadening. Under the right kind of leadership, a Department head can obtain fine cooperation and service from these people. In fact, the service rendered will compare favorably with that given by corresponding people in industry who have much higher salaries and work under a system of potent financial incentives.

There are some shortcomings in the handling of personnel in general by the federal government. The Secretary or agency head seldom devotes much time to general personnel policies because he considers these are functions of the Civil Service Administration. Whereas in industry the director of industrial relations generally reports to top management, in government the personnel director is several steps removed from the Secretary.

The situation would be improved if the Secretary could devote more time to matters of employee relations—to building up and maintaining the morale of the Department. In fact, it would improve management generally if the Secretaries had some say in the development of over-all policy and had more authority in personnel matters, such as granting salary increases for good performance.

In recent years business management has made good progress in the recruitment, training, and development of people for junior and higher executive positions and also in the training of supervisors. The progress has not been so rapid in government, although some steps for improvement have been taken in recent years, such as the Government Employees Training Act of 1958.

One important feature in the development of junior executives in business is rotation in different positions during their early years to determine the interest and special abilities of each individual. This method is more difficult in government because of the rigidity of Civil Service requirements in making transfers between Departments. Greater flexibility here, as well as revisions in Civil Service regulations which would permit the exceptional employee to be given faster promotion, would facilitate training and also improve personnel procedure generally. But even under existing regulations, government agencies should do more to institute programs for training supervisors.

A program was started in the Department of Health, Education, and Welfare a few years ago under which the entire Department is screened periodically to identify the younger people with the greatest potential for development. These people, along with some directly from college, are given a series of rotating assignments which will ensure a breadth of experience and an opportunity for growth. The program is working well and such a program should be adopted more widely throughout the government. This is an important step in preparing individuals to replace older persons in the top Civil Service positions who retire or leave.

There is a need for more career administrators with ability and broad experience to provide strong support for the political appointees in their development of policy and reaching decisions. I recall two or three such men who had wide experience in several bureaus, who had developed great interest in and knowledge of government policies, and who were quite objective in their approach. I found them very helpful to me. Many, however, have reached these top positions, where they could provide such assistance, with only specialized experience and training. An improved system of recruitment, training, and effective development would remedy this situation.

THE NEED FOR STAFF WORK
IN LOCAL GOVERNMENT

Although, up till now, I have mentioned only the federal government by name, I have not meant to confine my remarks to it alone. Annual expenditures of state and local governments, amounting to more than $55 billion, play an extremely important part in our economy.

The local governments, in general, have not kept up with either the federal government or business in improving the efficiency of their operations. One reason for this has been the lack of adequate staffs to assist the elective officials in administration. This probably has been due to pressure on the budgets for operating services.

Some progress has been made in the use, for instance, of local planning boards, but as a rule they are concerned with the planning of streets, zoning regulations, and the like. Often local governments also appoint advisory committees to study specific problems, but these efforts are generally haphazard.

Staffs to collect and analyze problems, both immediate and long-range . . . to present proposals for meeting these problems . . . and to assist the officials in arriving at decisions, can be just as helpful in local governments as in the federal government or a large business organization.

Some cities have found that a bureau of municipal research can perform some of these staff functions and be of much benefit to the officials. In some cases the bureaus are financed by the city or county government, but under these circumstances the officials all too often use them primarily for immediately pressing problems so that they do not have the time or resources to devote to long-range problems. The most successful bureaus have been those which are organized on a non-partisan, non-profit basis, with funds being furnished by the general public.

Such a bureau, the Rochester Bureau of Municipal Research, was organized by George Eastman in 1915 and during the early years was financed entirely by him. Since his death the funds have been collected from about two hundred companies and individuals. This bureau has had an outstanding record.

Its charter states it is a "non-partisan and scientific agency of citizen inquiry to promote efficient and economic methods of administering the affairs of local government in Monroe County; to collect, classify, analyze, and interpret facts . . . to make such information available to public officials and citizens . . . to promote the development of constructive programs."

Over the years, the bureau has been able to work closely with the city and county officials on a friendly, cooperative basis. Most of the studies have been conducted at the request of public agencies, but the bureau is able to exercise free choice as to the priority of the studies and also the areas in which it might initiate studies.

The over-all direction of the bureau is in the hands of a board of trustees, composed of about twenty leading citizens. A full-time director, with a staff of men who have had training in public administration, statistics, etc., conducts the work.

The bureau makes a thorough study of a proposal and presents the facts and recommendations to the official in charge of the municipal department concerned. That official makes the decision regarding the recommendation and takes responsibility for carrying it out. Publicity given to the reports of the bureau is in the hands of the government official.

Over the years, the studies of the bureau have covered a wide range of subjects. In recent years they have concerned such topics as the consolidation of the functions of the city, towns, and county . . . a uniform method of assessment . . . salary schedules . . . long-range financial studies . . . consolidation of school districts . . . establishment of a community college . . . and improvement of police services.

127

Case Study—Consolidation of Health Services in Monroe County, New York. As a case study to illustrate the operation of the bureau, I have selected an investigation which resulted in the consolidation of the public health services of the city, county, and towns under a single health department.

The bureau first studied the possibility of consolidating these services in the early 1930's and made more recent studies in the 1950's for the Joint City-County Planning Committee. As a result of the bureau's recommendations, special state legislation was obtained to permit this consolidation. In March 1958 the Board of Supervisors of the county authorized the establishment of the health district and requested the bureau to submit a report outlining a plan for consolidation of the local health agencies into a county health department.

With the assistance of the local and state health officials, the bureau developed a plan. Its report covered the functions, staff, and costs of all the local health agencies in the county and proposed a plan of organization with a budget for the proposed county health department.

The plan was submitted to the board of supervisors on July 1, 1958. It was adopted by the board and put into effect two months later, with only minor modifications. This County Health Department consolidated the services of twenty-seven independent local health districts in the county and was an important milestone in the adjustment of local government to the expanding and more specialized requirements of the metropolitan area. The new plan has had widespread acceptance in the community and has improved the public health services.

The consolidation undoubtedly would not have been achieved if it had not been for the persistent activities of the bureau for a period of years. The bureau, because of its record of accomplishments in the past, was able to obtain the cooperation of the public agencies as well as the private groups which were particularly interested—the medical association, health association, and social agencies. The bureau's services were used extensively by the new department during the transition period and also as new problems arose in the publc health field.

In this example, we can see how the bureau assisted the Board of Supervisors to formulate a plan for consolidating the county's health services. Such information-gathering and planning functions are similar to those of the staff of a business firm. The bureau's second major purpose was to help to gain acceptance of the plan and to provide liaison with the operating departments. This work parallels what I believe is another major function of management staff in business.

One of the recently completed bureau studies is entitled "Municipal Purchasing in Monroe County." This study examined the administrative policies and unit prices of local governmental purchasing divisions in the county.

Policy weaknesses were described and corrective action recommended in such areas as (1) organization, (2) the use of the New York State contract system, (3) standardization, (4) warehousing, (5) procedures, (6) cooperation among purchasing agents, (7) "buy local" policies, and (8) municipally operated industries.

Unit prices were examined through a sample consisting of approximately 35,000 purchase orders written by fourteen local governmental units in Monroe County. Careful evaluation of this data led the bureau to conclude that substantial savings ($2 million per year) could accrue to local governments if they would cooperate on a county-wide basis in such a way as to take advantage of lower unit prices. The bureau therefore recommended a joint purchasing unit under the auspices of Monroe County to facilitate cooperative procurement of necessary supplies and equipment.

With a competent director, a bureau operating on a non-partisan basis can contribute greatly to the improvement in local government—particularly today, with the problems of expanding suburbs and the creation of large metropolitan areas.

7

THE BROADENING SCOPE OF
BUSINESS RESPONSIBILITIES

At the outset of this book, I observed that top managements have made very substantial progress over the past few decades in improving their process of decision making.

Contributing much to this progress has been management's increased use of staff work. A well-organized staff can do much in providing the chief executive with information and analyses to aid him in reaching decisions. By keeping a relatively objective point of view the staff can suggest the pros and cons of alternative courses of action and, in this way, serve as something of a "check and balance" for management. In addition, the staff can provide liaison between top management and the operating units and can assist on the follow-through of management decisions and policies. This becomes particularly important in a large, decentralized organization.

In these ways, staff groups have strengthened the effectiveness with which a chief executive can direct a large business concern. They have done this without assuming any of management's functions. The chief executive still bears full responsibility for making policy decisions and for providing personal leadership for the entire organization.

Another broad factor contributing to the progress of business management over the years has been the increasing sensitivity of executives to the public interest. In this area, however, there remains considerable room for further improvement.

Because of the great number of people concerned in one way or another with large business organizations, these organizations are becoming, in a sense, quasi-public institutions. It is apparent that management needs to become increasingly alert to the ways its actions will affect and be interpreted by each of the groups of people to which it has a responsibility—its share owners, employees, suppliers, dealers, and customers . . . and indeed the public generally.

The progress of our nation's economy depends on a more widespread understanding of the role of business in our society, and on enthusiastic public support of those policies which will contribute to advances in business. The basis for such understanding and support depends, first, on the soundness of management actions, especially with regard to the broad public interest, and second, on management's success in communicating the facts to the general public— in presenting them accurately and in an understandable way that can be readily identified with the public interest.

While chief executives of large companies will never have to operate in the goldfish-bowl atmosphere of government, they undoubtedly will have to become even more sensitive to external influences than they are today. Business executives need to keep the public better informed, not only of *what* they do, but *why*. This is a communications challenge of a high order. Yet this challenge must be met if business is to gain the kind of public understanding that can be translated into public support.

In addition, business leaders have a responsibility to take a more active interest in public affairs, particularly those on a state and national level. There is real need for chief executives to enter more into the discussion of important government policies and to assist government and other public agencies wherever possible.

In this role, executives must conscientiously maintain an objective approach—considering at all times what is best for the common good of the community, state, and nation. There is great need for executives who can offer the kind of statesmanship of a Bernard Baruch or Paul Hoffman.

Businessmen can offer particular contributions to the government by bringing in fresh viewpoints, not only as to government programs, but with regard to administration and management techniques. When businessmen accept responsible appointive positions, they can bring with them ideas based on their experience in working with informal organizations without rigid rules and rigid lines of communication. They can also bring ideas regarding effective training and development programs for executive personnel, as well as administrative methods for the effective use of all personnel.

On the other hand, businessmen can *gain* fresh viewpoints from such an experience. Of course, they can benefit from an increased knowledge of government organization and operations. But, in addition, they can pick up new ideas in such areas as the use of task forces to study problems and make recommendations ... the check-and-balance system of consulting many groups before reaching decisions ... the persuasion techniques so necessary in carrying out decisions in government ... as well as budgeting techniques, methods of dealing with the press, and the general use of staff in a large organization.

HOW BUSINESS EXECUTIVES
CAN ASSIST GOVERNMENT

With the growing complexity of our society, the administration of government is becoming more and more difficult. While much staff work can be done by the government's own full-time employees, of more value than large increases in the size of full-time staffs is responsible information and advice provided by people outside the government, by leaders in all walks of life. Certainly, the best thinking outside the federal government should be made available, and government officials must be able to gain confidence in the objectivity of such counsel.

Business executives and other leaders should readily accept requests for consultation. They can be very helpful on advisory boards and task forces to deal with areas in which they are competent. For example, they can play an important part in the establishment and functioning of a municipal research bureau which can make truly independent and objective studies of local problems. Equally important, executives can present their views about matters on which they are well informed to committees of the state and federal legislature, as well as the Executive Departments. While many businessmen have contributed a great deal in this way, I can see the need for much broader participation.

In their professional and trade associations, leaders should assume greater personal responsibility for the formulation of statements on important policy matters under discussion in the government. Obviously, special interest groups will be keenly aware of how changes in government policies will affect their members. But, at the same time, I think these groups can make broader contributions when they consider the point of view of the nation as a whole and search for constructive approaches toward the solution of pressing problems before the government.

The Committee for Economic Development represents a good example of an organization in which the top businessmen themselves spend considerable time on their policy statements, with the assistance of competent staff men and academic men from the universities. The objective of the CED is to determine private and public policies which will promote economic growth and stability in a free society. And to quote from its by-laws:

All research is to be thoroughly objective in character, and the approach in each instance is to be from the standpoint of the general welfare and not from that of any special political or economic group.

Large organizations find it necessary to designate certain staff persons to maintain contact at the state capitol and in Washington, to keep in touch with developments affecting their business. Sometimes these people are from the public relations staff and at other times from the legal staff. But, as I pointed out in Chapter 4, when it comes to conferring with top government officials and appearing before

Congressional committees, it is important that a high officer—preferably the president—take on these important assignments rather than turn them over to a staff man. I know from my own experience with Congressional committees the difference in weight attributed to his words. Businessmen as a rule make a mistake in not taking advantage of the opportunity to express their point of view when they have a chance to testify at hearings before Congressional committees.

Chief executives should become better acquainted with the key Congressmen and Senators, and particularly their local representatives, and not wait until they have an ax to grind to get in touch with them. They will find that these legislators are as anxious to gain the views of business people as of other groups. Businessmen are remiss in their obligations to their company and to business in general if they do not express their views.

An area where business management has made very notable contributions is in encouraging—by both word and example—the active participation by company executives, especially the younger people, in community activities, nonprofit organizations, trade associations, and the like. There are many examples where business people are taking an active role on school boards, hospital boards, social agencies, the community chest, the Chamber of Commerce, and other business organizations. Their participation is very important and could well be extended further. Company specialists such as accountants, statisticians, and engineers can be very helpful to local governments, for example, in the study of specific problems. Such work is not only of real assistance to the community but it broadens and helps to develop a sense of public responsibility in the individual himself.

A further area where businessmen can assist government is in obtaining junior executives for key positions. The training of leaders for government service is becoming more and more important. As in the past, most will come up through elective positions, but many of the top appointive positions will still be recruited from individuals in private life in the middle or latter part of their careers. We shall need more of the able young people to enter government service and a larger number of the top business and professional men to devote some period of their careers to service in the government.

Colleges and universities can help by attempting to instill in their students a sense of public responsibility. They can encourage more of their graduates to seek government employment and can try, at the least, to create an interest in public service that the graduates can carry with them throughout their careers.

Business management can help, as I suggested before, by encouraging young executives to engage in outside activities. This, preferably combined with government service early in their executive careers—perhaps in a part-time consulting capacity—would prepare a larger number of able men for important government positions later on.

In the final analysis, the effectiveness of any organization is directly dependent upon the caliber of the executives who assume leadership and make the decisions. And, in the administration of our federal government, where decisions affect each of us in so many important ways, the decisions ... and the executives ... must be our best.